Life-Centered Financial Planning

Life-Centered Financial Planning

*How to Deliver Value That Will
Never Be Undervalued*

Mitch Anthony
Paul Armson

WILEY

Published by John Wiley & Sons, Inc., Hoboken, New Jersey.
Published simultaneously in Canada.

For general information on our other products and services or for technical support, please contact our Customer Care Department within the United States at (800) 762-2974, outside the United States at (317) 572-3993, or fax (317) 572-4002.

Wiley publishes in a variety of print and electronic formats and by print-on-demand. Some material included with standard print versions of this book may not be included in e-books or in print-on-demand. If this book refers to media such as a CD or DVD that is not included in the version you purchased, you may download this material at http://booksupport.wiley.com. For more information about Wiley products, visit www.wiley.com.

Library of Congress Cataloging-in-Publication Data

Names: Anthony, Mitch, author.
Title: Life-centered financial planning : how to deliver value that will never be undervalued / Mitch Anthony.
Description: Hoboken, New Jersey : John Wiley & Sons, Inc., [2021] | Includes index.
Identifiers: LCCN 2020023649 (print) | LCCN 2020023650 (ebook) | ISBN 9781119709091 (hardback) | ISBN 9781119709114 (adobe pdf) | ISBN 9781119709107 (epub)
Subjects: LCSH: Financial planners. | Financial services industry. | Finance, Personal.
Classification: LCC HG179.5 .A578 2021 (print) | LCC HG179.5 (ebook) | DDC 332.024—dc23
LC record available at https://lccn.loc.gov/2020023649
LC ebook record available at https://lccn.loc.gov/2020023650

Cover Design: Wiley
Cover Image: Mountaineer's mountain © Brad Jackson/Getty Images

Printed in the United States of America.
SKY10021366_092420

To the memory of Dick Wagner, a true fiscal philosopher, who always challenged me to think from multitudinous perspectives about how money impacts all of us individually, as a society, and as a world.
Your voice is missed.

—Mitch Anthony

This is dedicated to the rebels—financial advisers with spirit—the ones who put their clients' lives first and money second; the ones with the courage and conviction to stand up and be counted. Your time has come!

—Paul Armson

Contents

Preface

I t's time to redefine what the chief *asset under management* really is. It's plain to see what gets the attention from the financial industry at large—the money.

Compensation is tied to the assets under management, and a company's values are tied to the numbers in aggregate. In the money-focused advisory world, lip service is given to building relationships, but the money is what matters most. Now is the time to turn that notion on its head.

The principles driving life-centered financial planning are:

A: Aligning means with meaning
U: Understanding what makes clients unique
M: Monitoring all life changes and transitions

Yes, these principles do form the acronym AUM (Mitch does admit to being an acronymaniac). How many times have we overheard advisers telling stories prefaced with, "I've got this $5 million client ... " and wondered to ourselves what would that client think if he or she were standing here listening to that prefacing characterization of the relationship. It's difficult to see who clients *are* when our eyes are so pragmatically tuned to seeing what they *have*.

Every client has a story, and it is our responsibility to discover that story and build a financial plan around that story. We might say that the true sum of this business is made up of *stories under management*. Advisers are like the financial director in the movie of their clients' lives. Financial directors need to know where their clients want to go, the settings that the next scenes will play out in, who the supporting actors are, and ultimately, how they want this story to end. Money is tied to this story, whether it be the story of the past, the present, or the future.

In this book we're attempting to paint a portrait in three sections that characterizes:

- How the financial profession at large and the advisory value proposition individually are undergoing rapid metamorphosis;
- How you can make the shift to a life-centered financial planning approach; and
- What some of the dialogues of the future will look like.

Change Isn't Coming—It's Here

The world has begun to get a taste for a transcendent form of financial planning that merges what matters most with the assets being managed. It's about discovering the intention and purpose of the person and applying the assets at hand to those intentions. Life planning, financial life planning, lifestyle planning, and life-centered financial planning are all descriptors being used to identify a planning process that is anchored to purpose and not just the purse.

We're living in a day when the world of financial services is either embracing this truth or scrambling to understand it because their preexisting value propositions have proven hollow and are no longer valued as they once were. Being a successful practitioner of life-centered financial planning hinges on nothing less than showing up as the best person one can possibly be and showing up for nothing more than a desire to serve a client's best interests. This new approach requires a new skill set—and a new dialogue. The conversations are not tied to transactions but instead to transformation—to the adviser/client relationship, as well as the profession at large.

We have been laboring on both sides of the Atlantic for the last decade or two to raise awareness around the need for a planning process that places life at the center. After meeting a few short years ago, we decided to yoke our efforts in the interest of accelerating the change that needs to take place. This book is one of the results of this partnership. We hope you find direction, clarity, and empowerment within these pages and become a beacon of purpose-driven planning in your community. One thing we know from experience is this: once you have tasted the fruit of the life-centered planning dialogue, you won't ever go back to the business-as-usual conversations that this industry has been tethered to.

One of the great rewards we have experienced in our lives is the feedback from financial professionals telling us *how much fun* they are having now—how meaningful, rewarding, and energizing the conversations with clients have become. Nothing could make us happier than to hear this from you as well.

There's a very practical side to all this envisioning of a better profession and raising the sights of the advisory world: the more you know your client's story, the deeper the connection you have, and the more your business is ultimately worth. One adviser recently told Mitch he had been buying practices from retiring advisers and had an epiphany that if those advisers had built life-centered planning practices, he would know everything he needed to know about each client. Instead, he's being handed only numbers and facts and faint sketches of insight into the individuals he'll be serving. When this adviser goes to sell his business someday, he will hand the acquiring party all the keys to success—a story of numbers along with a number of stories, deeply personalized for each client. There is appreciative value to be found in this approach.

Thank you for choosing to read this book. It is our hope that you find this to be a valuable resource—and that the values described herein grow in you both personally and in your practice. Nothing less than client outcomes are on the line.

Acknowledgments

I would like to acknowledge the "circle of life" for my literary career that includes this book as well. This circle begins and ends with Cindy Zigmund—both an insightful agent and a top-rank publisher. In between Cindy's work is that of my dutiful and devoted wife, Debbie, who scrubs and shines every sentence I've written. So far, this circle has brought 17 books to life in financial services. I'm deeply indebted.

I would also like to acknowledge my coauthor Paul Armson, who has demonstrated a refreshing esprit de corps since our first meeting. I'm grateful to be in the yoke with him.

Finally, I would like to acknowledge all the wonderful life-centered financial planners I've met around the globe who wake up every day with the singular goal of doing what is right for their clients and placing their well-being at the center. You're all helping to change the world.

—Mitch Anthony

Part I

The End of Financial Services as We Know It

Chapter 1
The Masquerade Party Is Over

I intend to live forever ... so far, so good.

—*Steven Wright*

It's easy to get comfortable with the way you're doing things, but it's dangerous. Imagine the feelings that horse traders had 110 years ago upon hearing about the "horseless" carriage. Their sentiments had to range from incredulity ("How can you pull a carriage without a horse?"), to cynicism ("Who's going to take a chance on this unproven contraption?"), to utter disdain ebbing into panic as they saw their once established trade go by the wayside.

Imagine further the horse traders' agitation and confusion as the new technology measured its capacity and effectiveness in terms of horsepower—and yet, no horses were involved: "How can a mechanical motor the size of a big dog have the propelling power of 100 horses?" We need not elaborate any further; we all know what happened. Smug in their role of providing a commodity (the horse), horse traders failed to realize that customers were more interested in progress itself than the means by which that progress appeared.

People will do what they must to expedite progress in their lives.

Presently we are deep in the labor pangs of a similar revolution in the financial advice business, but this one is going in a reverse direction—away from technologically driven results to the more organic version of progress. We are entering an age of advice where the chief algorithm is emotions-driven and the result clients are looking for transcends a number.

This phenomenon has been building for some time on the periphery of the financial services industry. In 2001, Mitch first introduced the term *financial life planning* in his book *Your Clients for Life*. He had reservations about the public coming to financial advice offices for "life planning" services—they were coming for financial advice. Adding the term *financial* to *life planning* did, in fact, make it more palatable, but we admit that after almost two decades of effort from us and a few others, the concept of financial life planning appears to remain on the periphery of the profession.

This slow transmutation is about to accelerate in a big way. What was on the periphery is moving toward the center, and what was in the center is being pushed irrevocably to the perimeter. Investments and investment guidance have been the nucleus of the financial advice business since inception. The center is now in flux. We describe the arc of the business as moving from the boiler room to the living room—from a sales-driven industry to service-oriented profession.

The financial services realm was founded by investment managers who simply wanted to peddle their products. The business was then reengineered by advice and planning processes that put the investment products themselves in a secondary or tertiary position in importance. We are now in the throes of the final stage of evolution for the industry—life-centered financial planning—where the context of how the money will be used in the life of the client can no longer be ignored or quarantined as a "soft-side" issue. Up until this point, the question driving the advice industry has been, "Do you have enough money?" This will now be the secondary question. The primary one will be, "Are you managing your money in a way that improves your life?"

To properly help clients answer this question necessitates a different skill set than what was required in the past. Just being a clever capitalist or student of markets is no longer enough. To be successful going forward means being both a service-minded professional and a student of financial behavior. Scripts for selling are being replaced by candid truth-telling. Relative investment performance reviews are being replaced by financial accountability dialogues. If being genuinely interested in others' stories and building authentic relationships is important, then the future is yours—and it will be far more welcoming for those who have a bigger heart for service than they do an ego for selling.

As of this writing, there are two very promising examples of this move toward life-centered financial planning. First, the XY Planning Network (named for its focus on younger generations), founded by Michael Kitces and Alan Moore in 2014, has grown at such an accelerated pace that it even caught its founders off guard. While attending their conference, we met young and middle-aged planners alike sharing some destiny denominators: a focus on serving, not selling; compensation for advice, not products; and a desire to learn how to be better financial coaches.

While many of the young planners attending were just beginning their businesses, others had established practices in their markets. The group shares a life-centered focus, and the majority of planners are off-loading investment advice as they recognize that this piece has been commoditized. The future of the profession is moving toward their ideology—and the average age is 37. You do the math.

The next example is the BACK2Y Conference (founded by Paul) where close to 500 advice professionals from 12 different countries attend, and where the atmosphere is electric with enthusiasm for the next stage of the advice profession. Mitch sees his coauthor as a visionary rebel who has refused to abide by business-as-usual in flogging products and calling it "advice" or "planning." The title of BACK2Y pretty much sums up the maypole around which these vibrant and energetic advisers rotate—going back to "Why?" by asking, "Why are we in this business?" and "Why do people need the money?"

Time with these two groups and others that are emerging have affirmed our suspicions that the ROL™ (Return on Life) revolution is clearly under way—and it's not going back to the days of horse trading (we'll talk more about ROL in chapter 2 and throughout the book). The horse trading in our analogy is the business of investment returns and investment management (which is necessary but no longer deemed as valuable). As of this writing, the *race to the bottom* of fees for asset management is nearly complete with all the major firms capitulating to 0–.25 basis points for managing assets. Prices don't lie. They are indicators of perceived value. The wise professionals are letting others manage the monies while they manage the relationships. It is the horseless carriage that spells progress for both client and adviser.

For those who embrace the inevitability of the life-centered financial planning profession and the ROL revolution, it is important to understand the difference between evolution and revolution. Evolution is about waiting for the inevitable to take shape and for what is to morph into what shall be. Revolution takes place when those already convinced decide to hasten the pace of the inevitable.

Life-centered financial planning is here. Life is the point, the objective, the logical conclusion, and the only context that counts for our clients. It's time to get our eyes off the numbers and get our ears on the stories. Progress matters to people—and is best measured by the impact their money has on their lives. If we aren't centered on understanding our client's storyboard, then we will certainly be left behind by "those blasted contraptions" blowing dust into our eyes.

Financial Advice in Flux

For the last couple of years as we've traveled the globe and addressed financial planning and advisory conferences, we have been telling audiences that the financial services profession is at a historic inflection point and that a radical and substantive shift in value propositions is required—immediately. This is not an overdramatization or a sensationalized siren. This is a reality check. A broadened skill set is now required, and there is no turning back to how it once was.

After making remarks along these lines at an FPA Congress in Sydney, Australia, Mitch was followed to the podium by Stephen

Glenfield, chief executive officer of the Financial Adviser Standards and Ethics Authority; Stephen informed the audience of 1,500 planners and advisers of how different their world has become. For example, a bachelor's degree or better is now required to practice in financial advice. Those who have been practicing for years without this level of education are now required to complete specific educational courses to qualify.

In Australia, the Future of Financial Advice reforms, introduced in 2012, were enacted to better align the incentives of clients and advisers. In Canada, advisers have been working under the Client Relationship Model Phase 2 (CRMP2), introduced in 2013. In the UK, advisers are adjusting their practices to the Retail Distribution Review (RDR)—a set of rules aimed at introducing more transparency and fairness to the investment industry.

"In the U.S., they have just introduced a fiduciary requirement to put your client first, but if you go back 15 years, the U.S. would normally be 10 years ahead of the world," said Jacqueline Lockie, head of financial planning at the Chartered Institute for Securities & Investment, a global body headquartered in London. "A lot of regulators around the world are now looking to the FCA [the U.K.'s Financial Conduct Authority] to see what they are doing. RDR really has had a positive impact on the U.K. advice market by helping the public see how they are paying for the advice they seek."[1]

In our discussions with advisers in South Africa, one key question being examined is, "Do you receive financial advice from an 'adviser' or an 'agent,' and what exactly is the difference between the two?" Once the RDR legislation is enacted in South Africa, registered financial advisers (RFAs) will be the only ones able to offer financial advice. According to the current version of the RDR, an RFA can be an individual or a company, but in both cases, its ability to provide professional, independent financial advice will have to be verified by an external source.

At the heart of the reform in South Africa is a set of rules on how customers should be treated—aptly called "Treating Customers Fairly." One of the rules (number 4) is interesting to note: "Where advice is given, it is suitable and takes account of customer circumstances." Back in the United States, the Securities and Exchange Commission's Regulation Best Interest rule is gaining traction and will inevitably branch further and deeper into the discussion of how advice is presented. It seems so obvious that it's hard to understand how financial advisers operate without doing everything they do in the best interest of their clients. Yet many do.

Expanding Your Reach

In his book, *A Whole New Mind*, Daniel Pink presciently states that the "value propositions of the future would be seated in the right side of the brain."[2] For financial professionals, this means that if key value propositions can be replicated by software, algorithms, and artificial intelligence, then they are at the mercy of the market and what it is willing to pay—which is decreasing each year. Commoditization relies on pervasiveness and standardization to flex its muscles. Once a program can achieve what advisers have been doing for their clients, advisers are at the mercy of the going price of the technology. Asset allocation, rebalancing, fund selection, and comparative research are a few obvious examples of irreversibly eroded value propositions that once paid the bills for planners.

Exactly what is meant by a right-brain-oriented *value proposition*? Here are three examples of what might fill that void in our current quest for a more substantive value proposition.

Comprehension of Context

We have read from more than one brain researcher that the most immediate curiosity of the right brain when faced with any proposition or input is: How does this apply to me? How does it fit into my situation? We often ask financial planning audiences, "Have you ever prepared what you believe to be a comprehensive and applicable plan for clients, only to see them fail to act upon it?" Every planner is familiar with this frustration.

We suspect this particular phenomenon of inertia is that the plan is not properly anchored in your clients' stories. Knowing their numbers isn't enough. Clients don't feel the plan until they know you have heard and comprehended their story, which should form the core of the plan itself. Developing a plan based only on numbers and facts is like having all the bones in place, but the sinew, organs, blood, skin, and bones never coming to life. In similar fashion, the client's background—his or her current and unfolding stories—is the vehicle for bringing their plan to life. To expand your reach, you need to gain a broader understanding of your client's biography.

Narrative and Understanding

What kind of experiences have your clients had with money and investing? What have been their worst and best experiences? What kind of experiences, good or bad, have your clients had with other financial professionals? What kind of financial vicissitudes have they witnessed with their families and friends? How have these observations influenced their current perspectives? These are the types of queries we recommend (and will teach in this book) for enabling dialogue and building client narratives around their personal experiences and observations. We call it the *fiscalosophy dialogue*—seeking to understand clients' very personal perspectives on key financial issues.

Emotional Connectivity

Are your clients certain that you "get it" and "get them"? Everyone in the financial services profession purports to be in the "relationship-building" business, but let's step back and examine how relationships are built: they are developed over time and through trying circumstances in which people are able to demonstrate their commitment to others. Relationships are also built through the honest exchanges of our stories. Mitch's stories reveal what Mitch is about, while Paul's reveal what Paul is about. In that exchange, we find common ground—sometimes we stand on it for a lifetime.

It's not enough to be on friendly terms, which doesn't require emotional connectivity; a smile from a distance doesn't equal a firm and friendly handshake. Our gestures can mean the difference between "I can tolerate you" and "I'm really thankful for you." Far too many professionals are content with a peripheral comprehension and superficial rapport when much deeper and more profound connections are available. To expand our reach, we need to be willing to go deeper into the dialogue.

An adviser told Mitch during a trip to Johannesburg, "When I make clients my focus and not their money, and do everything in my power to understand them, their situation, and their future challenges, they don't come into my office and tell me they found something online that does what I do for one-third the cost." This adviser understands the relational value she brings—she worked hard to add it to her approach before she had to.

We are at a historic inflection point in the arc of financial planning and advice. What got us here will not take us forward. The machine-like advisory functions are no longer as profitable. The human functions hold far greater promise amid intensified scrutiny and advancing technology. The game isn't going to slow down in order for you to catch up—it's time to take your game to a new level.

Notes

1. Hope William-Smith, "Advice Around the World: Has Regulation Held UK Advisers Back?" Money Marketing, February 9, 2018. https://www.moneymarketing.co.uk/news/advice-around-world-regulation-held-uk-advisers-back/.

2. Daniel Pink, *A Whole New Mind* (New York: Riverhead Books, 2005).

Chapter 2
Erosive Value Propositions

I always wanted to be somebody. Now I realize I should have been more specific.

—*Lily Tomlin*

Do you find yourself arm wrestling psychologically with clients (or with yourself) over the actual value of the value proposition you sell? Are you moving from a transaction-based to a fee-based business and struggling to justify the new paradigm? Are you in a fee-based business and struggling to justify the reoccurrence of fees because the client fails to appreciate a value beyond the asset-management process?

The following story illustrates how a previously sold value proposition can haunt you.

Dave, an extremely successful adviser and admirable gentleman, called Mitch one morning and lamented, "I am so tired of these year-end meetings."

"Tell me about it," Mitch responded.

"Well, it's the same conversation over and over," he explained. "How did we do against this index? How did we do against this fund? How did we do against our neighbor who brags (and lies)? This conversation gets so old—year after year and client after client. It's like financial *Groundhog Day*" (alluding to the Bill Murray film about a redundancy gone mad).

"Dave," Mitch replied, "I have only one question for you: Who got this conversation started in the first place?"

11

"Ouch!" he replied.

"What has happened to you," Mitch offered, "is that you have fallen victim to the value proposition you sold in the first place. 'I can do better than xyz.' Now you're living with the reality of this value proposition. This particular value proposition, by the way, is unsustainable over time and ultimately causes major stress in every relationship when the tide turns against you."

Mitch then offered an analogy to this adviser by telling him he was thinking of starting a business called Mitch Anthony's Weather Advisory Outlook. "Bring me your calendar for the next year and circle the dates where you want to have an outing, go to a ballgame, picnic, etc., and I will do two things:

1. Look at historical weather records going back to 1920 and see how the weather performed on those dates.
2. Analyze your dates with a climatologic probability analysis program going forward.

After these analyses I will tell you whether or not it should be sunny or rainy on the date you chose."

The silence Mitch heard on the other end of the phone indicated that Dave thought the light on Mitch's front porch was flickering. "I take it that you're not interested in my business proposition?" Mitch inquired.

"I don't think so," Dave answered.

"Can you tell me what the difference is between my value proposition and yours? They are both predicated on factors we ultimately have no control over: the climate and the markets. Offering a value proposition around factors you cannot control is, at the very least, a formula for stress and frustration and at worst, predictors of burnout and insanity."

Many advisers are laboring in the yoke of an unsustainable value proposition:

- If you cannot control the outcome, it is unsustainable.
- If you cannot largely control client satisfaction, it is unsustainable.

- If the value of your offering continues to erode and the price being paid continues to fall, it is unsustainable.
- If your business model asks more and more of you and pays you less and less, it is unsustainable.
- If your business continues to threaten the balance in your life and zaps your enthusiasm for what you do, it is unsustainable.

Vacuous and Vaporous

From a global perspective, we believe we are at a one-of-a-kind inflection point in financial services, with value propositions that are either vaporous or vacuous.

A *vacuous* value proposition is something that sounds good on the surface, but there's really nothing there because technology and algorithms can do the same for nothing or next to nothing. Examples of this are asset allocation and rebalancing. There are plenty of companies now offering asset allocation and rebalancing for zero basis points, but you can't make a living on zero basis points. It's an empty proposition for the future of your business.

Chasing a number for a client is, in our opinion, another vacuous value proposition. Mitch often asks, "Do you remember when you were younger and you had a specific number in mind, thinking that if you could ever make that much money, then everything would be wonderful? What happened when you finally got to that number?" Nothing happened. Life just went on. Numbers actually mean very little. That's why chasing a number is a vacuous value proposition. What is meaningful is to explore how hitting a client's financial targets will impact their life. More on that later.

If chasing a number is empty, chasing a relative investment performance number is emptier. Comparing your results to an index or a competitor is meaningless and an exercise in futility. In fact, not only is it meaningless, it is erosive to your client relationships. Do you really want to be measured by factors you have no control over? Do you really want to start at zero value to the client at the beginning of every calendar year?

One of the things we emphasize is not to engage in comparative conversations because human beings are all on different paths. For progress to be meaningful, it has to be highly personalized. As soon as you start comparing what you're getting to what somebody else is getting, or what an index is getting, it's no longer about you. In chapter 12 we will introduce a method for deeply personalizing your clients' goals with their money and how to take all relative measures out of the equation.

By a *vaporous* value proposition, we mean those processes that are front-loaded in value and then seem to evaporate in value over time—namely, the process of financial planning. Most would agree that with the financial planning process, the heavy lifting is done early and that subsequent conversations are about *revisiting* and *reviewing* what was done in the beginning. This is where the value begins to vaporize.

If you are touting the value of a comprehensive financial plan and charging, say, 1% hinged to assets under management, eventually your client will begin to wonder, "Hmm, I saw all the work you did on the front end, and now we sit down and review performance and talk about the markets—and you're still charging me the same amount." Don't think clients are thinking this? Think again. "What have you done for me lately?" has and always will be the axiomatic truth that rules the realm of advice.

Sitting down with clients and reviewing what they've already seen on a statement does not constitute *advice*—it is simply a review of something you've already done. By the way, we also have a bone to pick with the idea of a "year in review." What is the point of looking backward when we have the option of looking forward? None of us can do a whole lot about changing yesterday, but we can do quite a bit about preparing for tomorrow. We need to shift the lens from *reviewing* to *previewing*. Try calling an annual get-together with clients a *forward planning meeting* or *year in preview meeting* and see if it impacts the quality and usefulness of the conversation going forward. Save the reporting on last year's results for the mail. This is about demonstrating value, not raising red flags around it.

To move to a model of transcendent trust we must offer value that is both self-perpetuating and sustainable. Each one of us can be that kind of adviser. We can and will do better. But to do so, we must thoroughly understand how this sector painted itself into the place it now stands in.

Very Brief History of Distrust

Financial advice is one of the world's least-trusted professions, even though there is an army of honest and well-intentioned advisers out there. One study on the most- and least-trusted professions in Canada had the following in the "least trusted" category:

Financial advisers
Religious ministers
Journalists
Mechanics
Taxi drivers
Lawyers
Real estate agents
Home-building contractors
Fundraisers
Politicians
Psychics (most distrusted)[1]

It's a very unflattering group of characters, and (especially as you're reading this book) we're sure that you would be more than chafed that there are people still in this profession giving off such an offensive impression. But they are out there, and the only way to lift the public view is by virtue of our character and our process being starkly distinguished from their approaches.

The concept of a financial adviser is fairly new. We suspect that much of the disparaging view is due to abstractions and confusion around what is labeled "financial advice." With accountants, bankers, brokers, financial planners, insurance reps, and investment advisers all calling themselves advisers, there is going to be a risk of getting grouped in with the group at large.

Not that long ago, specialists who went by a variety of titles had specific roles they fulfilled:

- Bankers sold certificates of deposits and loans;
- Brokers sold stocks and bonds;
- Insurance reps sold insurance products;
- Accountants sold tax advice.

Through legislation and industry changes, their roles began to overlap. For example, banks began selling insurance products, mutual funds, and bond funds. The waters continued to get muddier. Brokers sold sophisticated investment strategies and even loans. Insurance reps sold investment products. Accountants advised on how to grow your nest egg and protect it from taxation. The vast majority of these professionals began calling themselves *financial advisers*.

Why would someone need four different advisers, along with four different solutions?

The answer was simple: everyone had something to sell, and their income depended on selling a product—whether that product was a mutual fund, annuity, or insurance—all in the name of providing *financial advice*.

Approximately four decades ago, many financial professionals saw this tension for what it was, *a conflict of interest*. These professionals decided that a higher level of professionalism and integrity was required; hence the financial planning profession, as we know it, was born. These financial professionals actually did offer advice on financial issues such as investing, taxes, risk management, retirement, debt, and estate planning. Now you had advisers who actually were selling *advice*, not just products. But you also had many that were using the planning process as a more effective and less abrasive pathway to moving their products.

Over time the financial services industry at large began mutating from a commissions-based structure to one that charged clients a percentage of the assets they had to invest. Now, instead of being paid a commission by selling a client certain investments, financial advisers earned their fees based on the amount of assets entrusted to them, known as assets under management. Charging clients 1% per year of their assets has become the norm. The more a client's assets grew—or the more assets a client was *advised* to invest in—the more you made. There are also conflicts of interest with this approach as well, not the least of which is paying an adviser for simply managing assets instead of providing proper and holistic financial planning.

As a result, financial planning from a macro level has become more focused on gathering assets, or folding in products and services into the process, instead of what might be in the best interests of clients. Too many advisers rely on the value propositions of superior returns and outperforming the market. Some succeed for a short while, but most fail (as very few actually beat the market). It's an unsustainable value proposition.

Because of the focus on gathering and growing assets, it is tempting for an adviser to become more focused on a client's money than on the client. After all, don't people often behave the way they are paid to behave? This undercurrent has created a dynamic that has only served to perpetuate the lack of trust in financial advisers over the long run.

In our opinion, the money-centered approach just builds more distrust. We all know that people are more important than the assets they possess—it is essential that we employ a process that actually puts our clients' lives and their financial well-being at the center of the dialogue, instead of their assets. This is what our industry's value proposition of the future must guarantee.

As the first step in rebuilding trust, we encourage you to properly understand what transparency is and to demonstrate that transparency to your clients. That includes how much you get paid, how often you get paid, why you get paid, and what the value is you're providing to your clients. In chapter 4, Paul will introduce a powerful method for showing clients the value you bring and how to get paid properly for that value.

There is a huge difference between transparency and disclosure. Disclosure is what you have to do because it's been legislated.

Transparency is what you choose to do because you don't want any mystery or opaqueness in your relationship with your clients, and because it's ethically the right thing to do.

Change Your Mindset

Reappraising your value proposition will be the key to success, as the profession evolves and adapts to changing client expectations. The processes and value proposition that planners present to their clients has to become more personal and personalized. And for that to happen, we have to realize that your client's story and journey are more important than his or her numbers.

It's not about a story of numbers, it's about a number of stories that tells us where a client has been, where they are today, and where they are headed, as their story and life unfold into the future. So, if you want a value position that sticks, it has to resonate with the life and the soul of a client.

Today's clients want more from you than being a purveyor of products or an asset allocator. They can get these services elsewhere—and at a much lower cost. By becoming a life-centered financial planner, you can demonstrate your wisdom, experience, and insights, and help your clients clarify their life transitions, priorities, and goals. You already have the tools and the skills to make a difference in their lives.

For clients, money has purpose and intention tied to it. But as a planner, if you don't understand the purpose of that money, then you are really just operating in a black hole. Instead, we urge you to change your central value proposition to one that is focused on the life of your clients—Return on Life™ (ROL).

The definition of ROL is to get the best life possible with the money you have. You don't need to be a megamillionaire to have that life; you just have to have wise money management. We believe what consumers are desperately in need of is wisdom and guidance in their financial decision-making. And that's what the true definition of advice is. It's not selling a product or a process—it's selling wisdom and guidance.

When your value proposition is tied to the well-being of your clients and the financial freedom that allows them to do what they want, at the pace they choose, and with the people they want to work with ... well, you've got something that is powerful and attractive at a deep level.

Tracking Your Client's Life

To create a self-perpetuating value proposition, Mitch has developed a process called *Financial Lifeline*, where a planner collaboratively works with clients to chart out the next 15 to 20 years, including all the life transition changes that are likely to occur during that period (e.g., children leaving home and career changes). These changes are all charted out on a client's personalized lifeline. This process demonstrates to clients that it's better to prepare than repair. If we wait for these events to happen, then we're going to be left cleaning up the financial mess of our clients. But if we are proactive and prepare ahead of these events, we can ensure our clients are in much better shape, both mentally and financially, when they do occur. It's also true that the biggest financial mistakes people make tend to happen during these life stage transitions, when emotions run high and life is unsettled.

Mapping out a client's lifeline over the next 15 to 20 years allows the planner/client relationship to take on a highly personalized and very real human aspect. It's an excellent way for you to engage more closely with your clients around key life stages, thereby providing a more tangible value proposition. We'll touch more on this theme in chapters 7 and 13.

By making financial planning a more personal and life-centered offering, we believe planners can take the first step in rebuilding trust that has eroded over recent years due to industry misconduct. To us, it's a no-brainer. However, we honestly believe you can't rebuild trust with an industry, you can only rebuild trust with an individual. It all comes down to how you, as a planner, show up to work as a human being, with integrity and genuine interest in your clients' well-being. That's a value proposition that will never go out of style... and never get commoditized.

Note

1. "Financial Planners Least Trusted Professionals?" Wealth Professional https://www.wealthprofessional.ca/news/industry-news/ financial-planners-least-trusted-professionals/174411.

Chapter 3

Deprogramming Advisory Magical Thinking

This might be the strangest industry I've ever observed. It starts by making a promise it can't keep and sends out a statement every three months to prove it.

—Mitch Anthony

If you've been in the financial advice realm for very long you may be in need of what we refer to as "cult deprogramming"—the purging of ideas around advice that are impossible to deliver on over time. There are three common traits in adviser/client dialogues:

1. Prognosticating next year's financial climate
2. Executing perfect timing
3. Having to perpetually outperform last year's—or someone else's—returns

In fact, all three are simply traps advisers are setting for themselves.

Think of the risk in this pattern of advice. First, we're going to try to predict what will happen next. Second, if something acute does take place in the markets, we're going to execute perfect timing and make the exact right move at the exact right time. Third, we're going to outperform everyone else year in and year out. No wonder client incredulity is spawned as a result of such foolhardy attempts at "advising."

21

The consequence for continuing such conversations is eroded client confidence—and ultimately, career sabotage. In this chapter, we'll discuss how you can position your advice around what you *can* control instead of focusing on what you cannot. You don't have to play the wizard; you need only to play the guide.

The Crystal Ball

How often does a client look at you and ask, "What do you see happening in the markets in the next year?" Keep in mind that the advisory sector has encouraged such questions in the past because this was where they were placing their value—on soothsaying next year's developments. If you answer this question, on what basis do you prognosticate? An article you read by a so-called expert? The latest opinion of your favorite pundit? All we can say is, "God help you if you do." For years Mitch has been humored by a magazine popular with advisers that starts every year with their "prediction" issue, interviewing the same group of economists that they interviewed the year before—and who were largely mistaken in their previous predictions. These market prophets may lack foresight but they do not lack certitude.

According to data reported in the *New York Times*, forecasts are consistently off, often by a staggering amount. Since 2010, the data showed that the Wall Street consensus forecast in late December was wrong about the basic direction of the market 30% of the time. We could all get a 10% better result with a coin flip. Heads, the markets go up. Tails, they go down. Mitch has also been suggesting to some fund management company that is giving away tchotchkes at financial conventions to produce a crystal ball with their logo on it that advisers could utilize when the conversation comes up with a client. Here's how it would work:

Client: What do you see happening in the next year?
Adviser: Hang on for a moment.

The adviser then pulls out the crystal ball, stares at it mystically six to eight seconds, and continues: "This quit working back in 2008. I have no idea what is going to happen in the markets in the next year. Would you mind if I asked you a similar question? What do you see happening in your life and career in the next year that could impact you financially? That I can help you with."

Indiana Jones and the Temple of Doom

To execute perfect timing, you only have to know two things: exactly *what* is going to happen and exactly *when* it's going to take place. We're hoping that if you're reading this book, you've abandoned all such "superman" attempts at adviser prowess. Before the great recession of 2008, Mitch talked to an adviser who was trying to placate his concern about market irrationality. He told Mitch that he needed to take a serious look into "non-correlating asset classes"—meaning when the markets went down these particular assets typically went up. Mitch decided to heed his advice. Guess what happened next? That's right, the non-correlators decided that this was the year to correlate. Everything went down together. This is just one simple example of trying to outsmart the world with timing expertise. It is eventually going to get exposed because we don't know the times ahead of time.

Featured in Michael Lewis's book, *The Big Short*, John Paulson predicted the impending housing crisis, but almost lost everything in the process because he was too early to the move. Seeing what could or should happen—and knowing when they will happen—are clearly two separate matters.

RIP Comparison

Comparison is the death of joy.

—*Mark Twain*

Anchoring your value in relative investment performance (RIP) against competing funds, indexes, and more is a mistake. Comparative returns just aren't that helpful to anyone involved: your client, yourself, or your company.

Comparative results make for a very flawed yardstick for measuring a client's progress financially. It is not how they are performing against some outside measure, but rather how they are performing against their personal potential that matters most. What they are doing to hasten their progress is the first order of business. How the markets performed is a subsequent conversation to the first.

Imagine overhearing a conversation between a parent and middle-schooler, where dad explained his expectations as follows: "Son, the average boy in seventh grade in America had a GPA of 2.85, and you had a GPA of 2.75. I only want you to prove that you are better than the average."

Here are the questions that come to mind when we hear this:

1. What does the average have to do with the individual in question?
2. Will this number become a distraction from the work and development that really matters?
3. Shouldn't the focus be on what this student is *capable* of?

The conversation then moves to what measure—if not comparative returns—you could or should use to gauge progress with your clients. This is an arena of thought and dialogue that needs to be transformed in the planner/client relationship. The issue is *personal progress*, and by *personal*, we mean that each client's progress is unique. For Paul, it might be ramping up the risk management aspects of his financial life. For Mitch, it might mean finding ways to distribute more income toward charitable causes he is connected with. For someone else, it might be about reining in expenses.

Progress is, by definition, a very personal issue because progress cannot be measured without first taking inventory of where you are now and where you would like to be in the future. The common dialogue in financial services has mistakenly placed more emphasis on where clients would like to be than on where they currently are, and that's a detriment to them. Could it possibly be that clients have unrealistic expectations on future returns because they are being unrealistic with their current cash flows and spending habits? We're not sure the two are directly connected, but we have our suspicions that some of the pressure being transferred to advisers is the result of neglect and denial with current fiscal management. Progress is impossible to gauge without a clear picture of "where we are at."

We will deal in depth with this topic in Chapter 10.

> Gulliver describes a royal personage inspiring awe among the tiny Lilliputians because he was taller than his brethren by the breadth of a human fingernail.
> —Jonathan Swift, *Gulliver's Travels*

Where did this comparative measure concept originate?

It's difficult to deny that it most likely is *an idea rooted in arrogance*—at some point, some fund manager or fund company looking at the average returns said, "We can do better"—and they may have done better for a while. In a recent Standard and Poor's (S&P) study, "Does Past Performance Matter? The Persistence Scorecard," only 2 out of 2,862 broad domestic funds stock funds were able to outperform their peers by remaining in the top quartile of funds over five consecutive 12-month periods. Almost 100% (99.9%) of the managers that attempt to prove superiority fail over time. Those don't sound like good odds for anchoring a financial relationship. All we can say for the S&P index is that it makes a poor standard by which to measure progress.

We also suspect the comparative return conversation is grounded in greed—competition for assets under management leads many advisers to purposely sow dissatisfaction with a prospect's current investment result in order to have them transfer their assets to their practice. In doing so, not only are they acting in a less than prudent manner, they are making a promise that is impossible to keep.

It is not just the common practice of comparative measure that is problematic for the adviser/client relationship. Other mistakes in the measure mythology include:

Predicting the future by looking backward. This is projecting how investments will perform tomorrow by viewing yesterday's activity. Just because some baseball team's ace pitcher has been lights out in his last four appearances doesn't mean he isn't going to bomb in his next outing or get injured. Do track records matter? Of course, they do. But should you be held responsible for the unexpected? Of course, you shouldn't. Veteran planners know it's worth their time to explain to clients that they are not clairvoyant and that what happened yesterday is generally a poor indicator of what will happen today and tomorrow. Every fund has the disclaimer that "past performance is not an indicator of future results"—and yet many advisers continue projecting into the future based on data from the past five years.

Measuring against broad market patterns instead of specific and unique client needs and wants. The opportunity for solidifying the relationship exists in measuring *for* and not against. "What return do we need, and what amount of risk can we tolerate for *your* specific situation?" is a more applicable measure than measuring how you did against such and such an index. By measuring returns based on client needs and capabilities we are measuring what matters most and are, by virtue of life transitions, measuring dynamically. What kind of return your clients aim for will change as their life situation changes. Another key link in the ball and chain that is comparative measure has placed far too much emphasis on the quantitative aspects of progress and not enough on the *qualitative* ones. We'll discuss this more in chapters 12 and 13.

Wouldn't it be prudent to anchor your value in factors you can genuinely control and impact over time, rather than forces over which you have minimal control? So what if your strategies beat the indexes this year? If you hang your hat on it, your head will be on the line next year as well.

We're not suggesting that you should bypass or ignore the quantitative measure altogether; but we are suggesting that when you do measure numbers, it must be a more *personal* number that you are aiming for. We need to find ways of measuring progress that are not tied to forces we cannot control.

Mitch has no plans to ever retire, is helping to support both parents, has one child in college, one in the mission field, and one who just moved back temporarily to relaunch his career. What rate of return makes sense for him? Or, does a rate of return conversation even matter here? More relevant is a planning conversation about how many financial obligations and opportunities he is trying to balance. Another pertinent conversation would be how much risk he is willing to take with capital that is earmarked, for example, for his parents' support. These are conversations that will matter to him.

Mitch's life situation is different from Paul's. Your life situation is different from ours. Your obligations, goals, challenges, and opportunities make up a very personal portrait requiring individualized attention to detail. Your rate of return aimed for in your personal situation is probably not going to be the same as ours. There is also a very good chance that your client's "number" is going to be found in the balance between meeting obligations and staying on track with goals. A script for getting properly positioned with clients might go something like this:

Mr. and Mrs. Client, for years this profession has measured progress by comparing your returns to the S&P Index. If it was better than the average, we were successful, and if it was lower, then we were not. We've come to the conclusion that your personal financial situation has very little to do with some index out there. What we want to do is measure your progress at a very personal level. This means we want to make sure we're assisting you to make wise decisions in all financial matters. If there is a number we're going to shoot for, it's going to be a number that helps you stay on track with your goals without subjecting you to unnecessary risks. The only number I'm interested in is one that helps you make personal progress.

Personal financial planning requires personalized measures for progress. How you go about calculating this number is a work in progress, because it's hinged to life transitions and changes in scenarios that never sit still. The rate of return you and your client agree to pursue isn't as important as the fact that you are unfettering your practice from the shackles and chains of comparative returns.

We recently talked to a financial planner whose firm has begun using a system that monitors what clients said they would save, how much they did save, and how this discrepancy was going to impact their plan over time. The first time he used this report with a client was on the heels of having just discussed that client's returns. The epiphany that both this planner and his client had was that the monitor numbers were much more relevant than the returns number. This sort of process is a window into the future of financial planning and, we hope, the beginning of the end of the comparative measure being used in client conversations.

Think about our earlier example of a father discussing performance with his middle-schooler, and apply that to your own clients:

1. What does the average have to do with the individual in question?
2. Will this number become a distraction from the work and development that really matter?
3. Shouldn't the focus be on what this client is *capable* of?

Good track coaches have a practice of getting runners focused on their *personal best*, not on beating state records. The reason is, if the athletes are focused on some unrealistic number "out there" they are easily discouraged. But, if they are focused on constantly improving their personal best, they will maintain their focus on every little adjustment they can make to improve their performance.

You would do well to follow this example and get your clients' minds—as well as your own—off industry averages. Instead, place the magnifying glass on establishing personal bests in overall financial performance: spending, saving, protecting, investing, and giving. The best measure of success is knowing we have run the race well.

Chapter 4
Misplaced Value

The first step in dehypnotizing yourself is to realize you've been hypnotized in the first place.

—*Richard Bach*

The financial services industry has a vested interest in keeping advisers' attention focused firmly on the money—financial products and investments—because, overall, that's how the industry makes its money. The product providers and investment houses have huge advertising and marketing budgets to get and keep your attention. Plus, they have a powerful ally: the financial trade press—or, as Paul likes to call it, "financial porn." Ever notice those annoying pop-up ads? The attention-grabbing, click-bait email headlines? The financial industry has a lot to answer for. Does it even care about your clients, or is it only interested in your clients' money?

It's not surprising why so many advisers have created a service proposition that revolves around the money. The industry, in many ways, forced them down that path.

But the world is changing—fast. We can no longer provide a service to clients that revolves around what the industry wants: distribution. If we want to keep getting paid in the future, we have to deliver a service that focuses totally on what clients want. And most clients we've met don't necessarily want financial products. They may need them, but the reason for using them had better be aligned with their life situation.

So, what do clients really want?

Over the last 10 years, both in the UK and elsewhere, Paul has presented to thousands of leading financial advisers via various workshops, seminars, and conferences. These are designed for advisers who have the good sense to want to move their businesses toward a client-focused, fee-based financial planning service. They are moving away from the commissions-driven, product-focused, sales-based approach that has sadly resulted in financial services *not* being the most trusted profession.

However, even when Paul asks a group of these cutting-edge advisers what they think their clients really want, he's often astounded by the replies: what they *think* clients want is "a trusting relationship with their adviser" and for their adviser "to be well qualified and experienced."

This is where Paul points out that these are not things that clients want. These are things clients *expect*. Clients expect you to be well qualified, don't they? They expect to be able to trust you. They expect to be given the right recommendations. You don't say, "I always use this doctor because he always gives me the right medicine!" You *expect* to be given the right medicine. And that's how it should be with financial advisers. Yet it's amazing how many advisers dedicate numerous pages of their websites extolling these very things.

With a few more hints, advisers eventually tell Paul what clients *really* want: "peace of mind, financial security, and financial independence." That's more like it, don't you think? Or, is there something more important? In fact, there is some "thing" that is so incredibly important that it actually *determines* peace of mind, financial security, and financial independence. It's something *really* important, but before we tell you what it is, we'd like to demonstrate something to you.

Becoming Financially Independent Is Easy

We can show you how to become completely financially independent just about immediately. In the process, we can also show you how you can have total financial security and peace of mind. Just follow these five steps:

Step 1: Sell your car, or sell your house, assuming you have one.

Step 2: With the proceeds, get yourself a cheap flight to Kathmandu, Nepal.

Step 3: Take a short, cheap internal flight out of Kathmandu to Lukla (you'll enjoy the landing experience).

Step 4: Pop on your walking boots and head north. You'll eventually come to a little village called Jorsalle on the west side of the Dudh Kosi River, just south of Namche Bazaar, in the spectacular Khumbu region.

Step 5: Take a right turn. You'll now be off the beaten track. After another 30 minutes, you'll come to another little village—your new home! Here you can buy yourself a little shack for next to nothing. What's more, with most of the sale value of your car or house still in the bank, you'll probably be the richest person in the village.

There you go. You're now set for the rest of your life. You may have to walk half a mile or more for your water, but you *will* be financially independent for the rest of your life. You will also have total financial security—and you'll also be in what some would call a perfect place to find real peace of mind. This is how easy achieving financial independence can be.

Ah, you say, "What? I have to walk half a mile for my water? I'm not so sure about that. And what about my car? I like my car, thank you very much. I don't want to go without that. And what about my golf club membership? What about my high-tech music system? I can't listen to my favorite music on anything less than my top-of-the-range Bang & Olufsen."

Suddenly, what was easily achievable now becomes a lot more difficult. The price tag of financial independence has just gone up because of just one thing: *lifestyle.*

Here's a fact: When it comes to planning our clients' financial futures, the most important factor is the cost of their current and future desired lifestyle. That's what makes or breaks any financial plan. Although it is glaringly obvious, lifestyle is the one factor most often overlooked, even by financial professionals. Many advisers pay lip service to lifestyle and expenditure—too keen, perhaps, to get to the investment conversation.

Quite simply, a big lifestyle can mean a big problem, while a little lifestyle can mean a little problem: a big lifestyle requires a big number; a little lifestyle a lesser number. Think about it. Lifestyle is everything. It's what you live for. It's what you bust a gut for every day, in order to create a better life for you and your family. Lifestyle is the way you choose to live your life, or the way you choose not to.

Lifestyle is identifiable. It's what you do, and it's about what *you* want to do. It's also about what you *don't* want to do, and what you will pay to avoid doing those things. After all, that's why you have a private jet, right?

It's the cost of your holidays in the Maldives. It's the cost of your housekeeper or nanny. It's the cost of your gardener. It's the cost of your tennis court and swimming pool and their ongoing maintenance; it's the cost of privately educating little Tommy and Theresa at the private school. It's the cost of your flying lessons and the restoration of your vintage luxury car.

That's a pretty ritzy lifestyle just described there, but for some clients that is the lifestyle they desire, so it must be planned for.

Or, it could just be the cost of living a simple life in New York—or in Nepal. Lifestyle is *the* issue. Think about it. It's the only thing that anybody wants—and it's the only thing they want to keep (apart from their health). What if you could make that one thing the very focus of your service?

This is exactly what Paul did. He created a service proposition called Lifestyle Financial Planning. And for the last 10 years he's been helping other advisers adopt this service with his *Inspiring Advisers 7 Step Success System*. Lifestyle Financial Planning is financial planning with an end in mind. The end is a better life for your clients—and a better life for you too.

That one thing, lifestyle—the only thing that clients want—is the very thing you should focus your service on. What if all your focus, energy, and communication was directed toward understanding and helping clients achieve their desired lifestyle? It's the thing that the most successful life-centered financial planners focus on. They've made it a habit.

The focus of their service is not about their client's investments. It's about helping clients identify, achieve, and maintain their desired lifestyle without risk of running out of money—or dying with too much. It's about helping clients *get* and *keep* a great life. Lifestyle is what we work hard to achieve. Lifestyle is what we want to enjoy. Lifestyle is what we want to maintain and improve.

Of course, lifestyle is different for everybody, and that's what makes our job interesting. Lifestyle could be sailing a yacht around the world, simply being able to live a comfortable life, being able to gift to good causes, or perhaps creating a foundation that lives on after someone is gone.

Our job is about understanding clients and then helping them identify, achieve, and maintain their desired lifestyle, so they end up with a life worth living—a life well lived. That is what we should be doing for people. Instead, because of industry pressures, many advisers default to focusing on products and investments. They have misplaced their value. And they will lose in the years ahead.

Change Your Focus

Lifestyle Financial Planning is the ultimate life-centered financial planning service that is easy to demonstrate and deliver to clients. When you are dedicated to helping your clients get what they want out of life, encouraging them to do more, live more, give more; when you are focused on understanding their current and future lifestyle requirements, and helping them get and keep that life, clients can feel that your service is all about them. They can see that you are focusing on them, not their money. And here's the thing: because you are focused on your client's life more than their money, chances are they will trust you with all of their money.

Are You Embarrassed Easily?

You know the feeling: you're at a dinner party or some social gathering; everyone is chatting away, then suddenly it gets quiet, just as someone turns to you and says, "So, what do you do for a living?" Paul experienced this often and admits to frequently being embarrassed to call himself a financial adviser because of how the public often views them.

In the early 1990s, after Paul had been delivering Lifestyle Financial Planning to clients, he attended a Michael Gerber (author of *The E-Myth*) workshop in London. Paul wanted to learn how to build systems and processes into his business. During the workshop, Gerber talked about the importance of understanding your customers and how surveys should be carried out on a regular basis. Gerber explained a caveat: Whenever you survey your customers, don't just ask the questions you want to hear the answers to. Ask questions you *don't* want to hear the answers to.

Paul returned from the workshop and composed a survey to send to his clients, and he didn't hold back. He asked them to answer questions about everything: how clients felt about how Paul conducted a meeting, the questions he asked, the software he used, the reports he created, the financial plans he prepared. He asked about the financial planning experience, about how Paul was remunerated, about how much he was remunerated. He asked about his offices, and even what clients thought about the car he drove.

Paul received some pretty interesting feedback. But one questionnaire came back that seriously disturbed him; it wasn't completed. Instead, Jimmy, one of Paul's favorite clients, had simply taken a thick blue marker pen and written all over the front page in caps: *"I HAVEN'T GOT TIME FOR THIS! CALL ME ASAP!!!"*

Paul was a little concerned that his questionnaire had upset Jimmy, so he nervously called him. Jimmy told him, "Paul, the reason that I didn't fill in your questionnaire is first, I'm busy. But mainly it was because I didn't get it! It was all about you as a financial adviser. But I don't see you as my financial adviser. I see you more as my 'life planner.' Yes, you've sorted my retirement plans and arranged my investments and my estate planning, and you've reduced my taxes, but what you've really done is you've helped me to plan my life. Without you I wouldn't have done the things you've encouraged me to do over the years, and I wouldn't be doing half the things I'm doing right now—all thanks to you. You're a life planner more than you are a financial adviser. But I'm guessing if you're going around calling yourself a financial adviser, you are mad! You are probably repelling more clients than you are attracting. You're not a financial adviser—you're a life planner. And I'm guessing that if you do for your other clients what you've done for me, then they will agree. Why don't you ask them?"

Paul took Jimmy's advice. He called 10 of his best clients and told them what Jimmy had said. Did they agree? Every one of them agreed.

Suddenly, Paul had a "light bulb moment." As Jimmy had intimated, he had been going around embarrassed, calling himself a financial adviser, when actually there was far more to his service than providing financial advice. But how could he communicate this to clients? How could he differentiate himself from advisers whose main focus was only selling products and investments? Thanks to Jimmy, he suddenly realized he wore three hats.

Understanding the Three Hats You Wear

Every great financial adviser wears three hats, even if they don't realize it. Let's look at each hat you wear.

The Third Hat: Financial Adviser

This is your least important hat—your financial adviser's hat. So, what is financial advice? Paul explains to clients that financial advice is anything to do with discussing, arranging, implementing, changing, or advising on any form of financial product or investment. This includes investments, asset allocation, portfolio

construction, risk profiling, rebalancing, insurance protection
(including life, critical illness, medical, and health), retirement
plans, annuities, and bonds. It also includes trusts, tax wrappers,
bed and breakfasting, tax loss harvesting, mortgages, loans, and
any form of savings. Paul explains to clients that all of this falls
under financial advice. Financial advice is not the same as financial
planning. These actions are things you do—if necessary—*after* you
have done financial planning. Clients get this.

The Second Hat: Financial Planner

The financial planner's job is to understand the numbers: identifying a client's current net worth and the assets they have. A financial
planner determines a client's liquid and nonliquid assets. To sum-
marize, financial planning means understanding a client's current
and future sources of income, including regular inflows and any
one-off inflows that might come into that client's life based on prudent assumptions. Financial planning is about expenditure: What
is the cost of their current and future desired lifestyle? What about
any one-off expenses they see coming? Financial planning involves
crunching the numbers to forecast where they are heading financially: Are they on course to run out of money, or could they die with
too much money? We'll discuss more on this topic in Chapter 16.

Of course, financial planning requires the use of decent software
to help crunch the numbers and to make prudent assumptions
about inflation, investment return, and longevity—all of which
must be revisited on a regular basis to help clients understand
what needs to happen to get and keep the life (and lifestyle) they
say they want. Financial planning is an ongoing service. In a way,
you become your clients' GPS—or, as we like to say, FPS (financial
positioning system). You keep your clients headed in the right
direction throughout life.

The First Hat: Life Planner

The most important hat you wear is that of a *life planner*. The life
planner's job is to find out where clients are right now in their lives

(i.e., their current situation), and how they got to where they are now (what's their story?)—and when you understand this, identify where are they trying to get to in the future (what do they want their future story to be?). Specifically, it's about identifying the sort of lifestyle they have now and the sort of lifestyle they want to enjoy going forward.

If you explain to clients that you do things differently than most advisers by wearing three hats in this order—life planning, financial planning, and financial advice (if necessary)—you will differentiate yourself and avoid the transaction trap of getting stuck talking about financial products. This process enables you to have engaging first client meetings where you focus on what matters most: your client, not their money. Clients can feel that you are more interested in them than you are in their money. This enables you to build rapport and high levels of trust because you are demonstrating your interest in them at a human level.

We've noticed that most advisers are very good at wearing the third hat because they've had years of practice. But many fall short when it comes to keeping the focus on what matters most by successfully communicating and wearing the first two hats.

You can adopt this three-hat approach to help communicate that there's more to your service than transactional. When you can explain to clients in the first meeting that the meeting is all about them—that until you know about them, you have no right to talk about their money or tell them what to do with it, you will differentiate yourself. You are now ready to engage in a genuine life-centered conversation where financial products and investments become simply the tools in your bag used if and when necessary to get the job done.

This approach is how you get clients to understand your real value. This is putting your value proposition in a proper place and order.

Chapter 5

The Bottom Line Is Not a Number

Not everything that counts can be counted, and not everything that is counted counts.

—Albert Einstein

Recently after a round of golf, Mitch was chatting with two acquaintances—a surgeon and a businessman who happened to have recently retired—about who their financial advisers were and what they did for them. They happened to have the same adviser, and both agreed that the primary value this adviser brought was "rebalancing." Mitch asked them to explain further, and one of them responded, "Every three to four months he rebalances our holdings to keep us on track with our investments."

These were two intelligent clients who had been convinced that paying their adviser to frequently check on their investments was a good idea and worth whatever they were paying him. Yet, there are numerous studies demonstrating just the opposite is true. According to Betterment data on login frequency, checking your portfolio quarterly instead of daily can reduce the chance of you seeing a moderate loss (–2%) from 25% to 12%.[1] We suspect it then stands to reason that checking on your portfolio annually instead of quarterly could produce the same dynamic. Our point is, the more clients check on their portfolios, the more often they stress about minor movements up and down, and the more likely they are to want to pull money out when they should be leaving it where it is.

We tell this story not for the sake of debating how necessary or how often rebalancing is to the process, but to illustrate the thin amount of value this adviser had sold to his clients. Because his focus was solely on the numbers, the adviser is basically playing his cards toward his clients' bias concerning loss aversion (that generally becomes even more pronounced in retirement). What happens when one day these clients find out that the rebalancing he does for them is an algorithm that can be done at a fraction of what they are paying?

What should the nexus of the adviser-client relationship and dialogue be? Is there a more profound anchoring point aside from the money mechanics—investing, rebalancing, and reviewing—that has been sold in the past? We believe there is. Although these mechanics will always be a *part* of the process, they are not *central* to it. The chief asset under management is the person in front of you, the story of what they hope to accomplish, and your ability to help them.

The Human Elements

As Daniel Pink so presciently pointed out in *A Whole New Mind*, the value propositions of the future are going to be rooted and grounded in the right side of the brain—meaning that it is the *human element* that people are going to pay for, and eventually everything else is going to become commoditized and erode in value. In financial planning, the human element is best expressed in the discovery and review processes. We could juxtapose the binaries of the advisory relationship as:

1. A story of numbers
2. A number of stories

If our central value is the story of numbers, we are consequently relying on functions that are easily replicated by algorithms and programs that are mechanized and programmable procedures. This is not the human side of the business Pink was referring to—and robo-allocation only verifies that fact. Any adviser whose value is being questioned at this point as a result of that disruption, clearly has been relying too heavily on automated processes and has not purposefully demonstrated human value.

The human aspect of the advice and planning process is found in your clients' stories: where they came from, how they got here, and where they hope to go. Knowledge and integration of these stories give the financial plan a visceral resonance and exponentially raise the probability of follow-through on a client's part. Why? Because when their story is the central context of the planning process, they *see themselves* in the proposed plan.

We've often asked financial planners how many of them have been frustrated after preparing a comprehensive financial plan, only to see their client choose not to act on that plan. Every hand goes up. We all know the feeling. Almost exclusively, the reason this happens is because the plan has been built around their clients' numbers instead of their story. Without a client's story at the center of the plan, all you have is a skeleton—a pile of bones without muscle, sinew, organs, or skin. And if the plan doesn't resonate with clients, they won't act on it.

The Central Question

If you want to change the dynamics of the financial relationship to a value that is most meaningful, start by changing the central question being answered in that relationship. The core question driving the advice and planning world has been, "Do you or will you have enough money?" It's no surprise that advisers then have to spend the majority of their time validating allocations, investments, and returns. The result is a never-ending cycle where advisers are forced to constantly justify how their clients are doing on a relative basis—and in the end, that's a game no one can win.

In the ROL paradigm, the central question is not "Do you have enough money?" That is a tertiary question at best. The central question is, *"Are you managing your money in a way that is improving your life?"* This places the emphasis on where it belongs—on behaviors that produce results. This positions the adviser to be in a seat of true advice where clients are weighing in with wisdom on the financial behaviors and principles needed to better their financial situation.

Change the central question you are attempting to answer, and the perception of your value will change with it.

One way to help your clients define what improving their life looks like is to ask this question:

> "Several years from now, what does your life have to look like for you to feel a sense of well-being, and that you're making progress, and have the freedom to live life the way you want?"

What you'll hear are the values that are most important to them—and you can start planning with those in mind. What you won't hear is, "I beat the S&P 500 by 100 basis points."

Building Relationships: The Roles You Will Play

The key to building lasting and inviolable relationships is to hone your skills on the human aspects of delivering advice. The financial services industry is at a crossroads between process and proper positioning—with processes going down the same drain of commoditization that products have already passed through. The real value of advice lies in improving your skills on the human side of this business.

People are complex, and we can't treat them as a soft skill add-on. The soft skills in planning represent the hard stuff.

Computers and algorithms can work out all the hard data and technical stuff. Planning is all about human connection; and that's something none of us can ever forget, if this profession is to remain relevant and vibrant in the years ahead. Two roles we'd encourage you to consider personally edifying are: (1) biographer and (2) fiscal philosopher.

A key to building relationships that last is the open exchange of stories and experiences between you and your client. This exchange also helps build trust and empathy in the relationship. It is essential that you become a better biographer of your clients' stories, as well as get better at sharing certain aspects of your own story. By doing so, your clients will be able to more effectively connect with you. In chapter 9, we'll look at the questions that will help you to become a first-class biographer of your clients' journeys.

The second key to building lasting and inviolable relationships is to become "fiscal philosophers." Fiscal philosophy means having a point of view. It means sharing the principles that you abide by and articulating these principles with conviction. Establish a clear *fiscalosophy* of how you personally deliver advice using the fiscalosophy dialogue we discussed in chapter 1. It's important for clients to know they are interacting with a financial planner who has a point of view. They want a professional who is informed by experience and who truly wants to help them make progress in their life. People will follow someone who has a point of view that resonates with them.

Here's an example of something you might say: "Look, everybody else might just be talking about your money and your investment returns, and yes, we will also talk about that, but that's not why we're here. We're here to help you get to where you want to be in life; to have the life you want to have. We understand your money has purpose."

It's all about opening up the financial dialogue with clients in the most meaningful context possible.

We strongly believe that financial professionals need to *earn* the right to talk to clients about their money—and that means taking the time to truly understand clients, including their pain points and objectives. Advisers need time dedicated to understanding clients' journeys: where they've been, where they're at, and where they're going. Only then do we earn the right to begin diving into the financial planning process.

If the bottom line is a person and his or her pursuits—and not a number—then you must take a good, scrutinizing look at the core tenets of the practice you are building. Do your processes and descriptions of what you do sound like everybody else out there in the noisy financial marketplace? Or have you found a way to stand out in bold relief from those just making noise and raking assets? We have provided the following Return on Life™ (ROL) Manifesto that you can share with your clients so they understand your approach.

Return on Life™ (ROL) Manifesto

Professional financial advice has traditionally focused on helping you make and save more money. But lost in the shuffle was, "What's the money for?" The Return on Life™ (ROL) philosophy says money is still important but shifts the focus to putting your life at the center of the conversation. It's about helping you live the best life possible with the money you have.

Here are the beliefs that constitute the ROL approach:

1. *Money is simply a tool.* Money is not the goal, and it is not an end. It is a tool that we manage—exercising caution and wisdom—for the benefit of improving our clients' lives.
2. *Comparative measures are neither helpful nor necessary in making progress.* How an individual's returns compare to any index, fund, or investment category (relative investment performance) are inconsequential.
3. *Progress must be personalized.* Progress is best measured against an individual's own potential. For measures of progress to be effective, we must first establish a personal benchmark. This requires knowing where money is coming from and where money is going.

4. *The primary measure of success is Return on Life (ROL).* The fundamental question in the ROL philosophy is not, "How much money do you need?" but rather, "Is your money being managed in a way that is improving your life?"
5. *How I am compensated is a matter of absolute transparency.* As a professional, I deliver value to my clients and make sure they understand what I offer and how I get paid.
6. *I can provide quality and value to a limited number of clients.* In order to serve others well by providing the greatest amount of value, and to keep my life in balance, I must choose to serve a reasonable number of clients.
7. *We are stewards of wealth, not owners.* Ultimately, everything I own will end up in the hands of others. With this understanding, I pursue stewardship that recognizes the responsibility of supporting and securing personal, family, and community life.
8. *The greatest value I can bring to my clients is to bridge their means with their meaning.* I recognize the unique role I play between my clients' means and their sense of purpose and intention with their money.
9. *I will not entrust my clients' well-being to anyone who does not put my clients' interests ahead of their own.* I understand the sacred trust that exists in financial matters and will never refer my clients to anyone who does not appreciate this elevated level of trust.
10. *An ROL Adviser has a calling, not a job.* I understand that my commitment, passion, and devotion to help people improve their lives through wise financial decisions is more than just employment. It is a vital service that demands professionalism and intellectual, emotional, and spiritual investment of self.

What We Need to Know and Continue to Know

In the ROL approach to discovery, we have developed inquiries that help us understand clients' perspectives formed by their experiences and observations, their intended payoffs (what they want their money to do), and their current position in life (what changes they are migrating through). These inquiries draw out the deeply human facets of the planning process as each step in the inquiry requires your clients to explain their view and tell their stories. In chapters 11 through 13 we will take you deeper into these dialogues and the tools required for processing each client's story.

Your Bottom Line

The great promise of the ROL approach to planning is not just about what it can deliver into your clients' lives, but also what it can deliver into the quality of *your* life. We know many advisers who are weary answering for markets and returns and events completely outside of their control. We know many planners who are tired of the same old, redundant conversations about money and yearly review.

The profession is moving quickly toward a much more profound focus on quality of life by helping clients get the best life possible with the money they have. This is the goal of life-centered financial planning, and we believe this is where the industry is headed. We believe that people want to manage their money in a way that improves their lives.

Is the financial services industry in an evolution or revolution? The difference between evolution and a revolution is this: If it's an evolution taking place, then it's just a matter of time. If it's a revolution, it's because some people have foreseen the eventuality and have decided to hasten the pace in that ultimate direction. We believe the direction is set and that the old way of quantitative advice is dying a quick death. Your clients require—and demand—more. The profession needs to deliver more. *Return on Life* and *Life-Centered Financial Planning* is that *more*. Return on Life is the central value that we deliver and Life-Centered Financial Planning is the process whereby we deliver on that value proposition.

Note

1. Dan Egan. "High-Frequency Monitoring: A Short-Sighted Behavior: If You Are Checking Your Portfolio More Than Once Per Quarter, You're Doing It Too Much." Betterment: September 16, 2014. `https://www.betterment.com/resources/high-frequency-monitoring/`.

Part II

Making the Shift
to Life-Centered
Financial Planning

Chapter 6

From Money Centered to Life Centered

She had grown now not to blame any man, honest miner or bloody bandit. She blamed only gold. She doubted its value... Could she ever forget that vast ant-hill of toiling diggers and washers, blind and deaf and dumb to all save gold?

— *Zane Grey, The Border Legion*

Around 20 years ago a new movement began taking shape on the periphery of financial planning. Originally introduced by George Kinder as *life planning*, and later reintroduced by Mitch as *financial life planning*, it has evolved into what we refer to as *life-centered financial planning* (or lifestyle financial planning). Instead of focusing on the clients' assets, life-centered planning puts their stories and their lives at the epicenter of the process. Life-centered financial planners believe the ultimate goal of money is a greater return on life—and the money is simply the tool or utility facilitated in that pursuit.

Because of how they approach their work, life-centered financial planners need to know as much about a client's story as they do about their finances. They need to understand the client's backstory and history with money; their present situation—and where the risks and opportunities lie; and their future transitions, prospects, hopes, and dreams. They need to know the kind of lifestyle the client is trying to achieve and maintain. The idea is simple but

Figure 6.1   ROI versus ROL.
SOURCE: Mitch Anthony.

profound: your client's money is there only to support your client's story.

Figure 6.1 has been used by many life-centered financial planners to properly position the client's assets in the life-centered process. The gerbil in the wheel represents the never-ending chase that the ROI approach demands of both you and your clients. The sailboat represents the idea that money is simply a utility—like a sail on a boat—that we skillfully manipulate in order to navigate. It's not the shore we're sailing for, the sea we sail upon, or even the vessel upon which we sail; it is only a utility that we adjust according to the conditions we're in.

We believe this life-centered approach to financial advice is the most advanced version yet to emerge. The result of this approach means that no funds or products need to be *sold*. They will be utilized only as needed and where appropriate. The underlying message of life-centered financial planning is that until an adviser knows about the client as a unique individual, they have no right to talk about their money or tell them what to do with it. With life-centered financial planning, life—not money— is at the center of the plan. After all, your client's money is there to serve them, not the other way around.

Figure 6.2   Return on
Life model.
SOURCE: Mitch Anthony.

The picture we are trying to paint here is *not* that advisers who focus on money are ill-motivated or suspect in nature. The key difference between money-centered and life-centered financial planners is that money-centered financial planners use *inferior processes* that treat money as if it were the most important factor in the equation. This is an important difference because those processes fail to account for the individual nuances and each person's unique story. Even good advisers using inferior processes produce inferior results. With Return on Life (ROL) at the center of the value proposition, the client's story becomes more important than the client's numbers. Why? Because the numbers are there to support the story, not the other way around. With ROL at the center (see figure 6.2), we let the client know that first and foremost, we need to understand their story and their situation—past, present, and into the future.

The historical model of financial planning (figure 6.3) places a dollar sign at the center of the proposition and moves directly into the six aspects of financial planning:

1. Asset management: the investment strategy piece
2. Tax planning: strategies for minimizing taxes
3. Risk management: protection of a client's assets
4. Cash flow planning: debt and spending
5. Distribution planning: strategies for retirement income
6. Estate planning: wills, trusts, giving, etc.

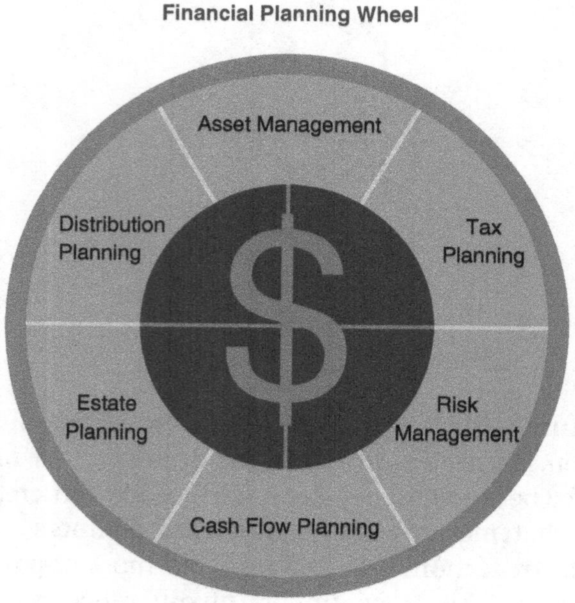

Financial Planning Wheel

Figure 6.3   Historical model of financial planning.
SOURCE: Mitch Anthony.

When done properly, this holistic financial process takes into consideration every aspect of a client's financial situation. What is the point of focusing only on investments and not paying attention to your client's levels of debt or spending, or not being properly insured against major losses? If we, along with our clients, continue to view their money through a singular lens, they will probably never reach the point of true financial independence.

The process of financial planning has historically been focused on numbers and how to make them work for clients over time. Cash flow analyses are often fundamental to the process. Advisers understandably want to know what their clients have—and how much they have. They also need to know their clients' debts and sources of income, and their savings and spending habits. Advisers also ask some *discovery* discussions to varying degrees, depending on their approach.

The blind spot in this approach is that advisers can create a highly personalized plan without knowing the stories and insights that *personalize* the client. Those stories are from the past, the present, and the unpredictable future. The superior process we speak of is a process that gathers and analyzes the stories before attempting to process the numbers—it's the "life" in life-centered financial planning.

It's All about Discovery

It is in the *discovery* phase of the planning process that we believe life-centered financial planners can do a much better job by adding true and lasting value. Why? Because life-centered planners understand that every person is unique—no two circumstances are exactly the same. The life-centered financial planner also understands that *discovery is never really finished*: people's situations are in constant flux and the wise adviser never assumes that any client's predicament is static.

Your client's personal journey—their defining experiences, their perspectives on money issues, and their particular situation in life—is uniquely theirs, and we firmly believe that cookie-cutter processes don't cut it. Many financial planning processes assume too much and treat all people as if they were the same, failing to account for individual circumstances and experiences.

Their story comes before the numbers—life-centered financial planners need to know the stories—past, present, and future.

The Past

How did your clients get to where they now are? What are their origins, their experiences with money, and how have their family and work situations evolved?

Did your clients grow up poor, middle class, affluent, or somewhere in between? What kind of lessons around money have they learned along the way? What has their financial journey looked like?

If they're like most people, they've had their ups and downs, good fortunes and bad. Are you aware of those specific incidents?

They've probably decided on some rules or principles for managing their financial situation that has brought them to where they are today. They've most likely had some experiences around investing and other financial professionals that stand out. Are you aware of their level of posttraumatic advice syndrome?

With life-centered financial planning, we view each client's financial history as critical to understanding them. History should never be ignored, glossed over, or trivialized because it is critical in understanding the unique individual you are working with. There is a reason that well-trained physicians start their discovery process with a thorough examination of your medical history—they understand it is the primary contributor to where you are today. Life-centered financial planners believe the same is true when it comes to financial well-being.

The Present

What is your client's current situation, both personally and professionally? What is their level of comfort and concern in the various parts of their financial life?

What does their family situation look like today? Is it in flux and experiencing some major changes? What is their current career status? Are they happy with the path they are on or are they looking to make some changes? Are they content with where they live, their life expenditures and what they get in return, their exposure to risk, and their protection of what they've fought so hard to gain?

Every person's level of satisfaction hinges on how well they are using the money they have toward the life they desire. Many people gather money hoping to *someday* have a life. With life-centered financial planning, a core value is helping your clients get the life they want when they want it. It's about helping clients get the best life possible with the money they have.

The Future

What are your client's long-term goals? Do they have a proactive financial plan for all of the major transitions unfolding in their lives? Are they prepared for the expected and unexpected events of life?

Life-centered financial planners understand that *money goes into motion when life goes into transition*:

- Having a child, going to college, getting married (or divorced)
- Starting a new job, becoming unemployed, starting a business, selling a business
- Retiring, traveling, dealing with health challenges, changing residences

These are all examples of life transitions that will have a major negative impact on your clients' financial well-being if not prepared for today. Remember, life-centered financial planners approach the future with the philosophy that it is *better to prepare than to repair*. They take the time to understand the unique personal and family situations and dynamics, and to plan accordingly—before these changes happen! The life-centered financial planner's goal is to see their clients live the life that they want to and address all the possibilities that could affect that life going forward.

Each client is unique, and life-centered financial planners understand that. A couple with a special-needs child requires a different approach than those with no children. A person who never really wants to fully retire needs to plan differently than someone who can't retire soon enough. It is sad to say, but there are many in the financial advice world who never bother to learn these things about their clients. We suspect that this is because their real client isn't viewed as a person but instead that person's money. If you don't understand your client's one-of-a-kind situation and the challenges they face, you may be giving them the wrong advice.

By looking ahead and anticipating changes, and being financially prepared for them, we help our clients avoid the mistakes that many people make while navigating through major life events.

A Tale of Two Advisers

Margaret and John are 58 and 59 years old, respectively. They both hold stressful public sector jobs, earn good incomes, and have final salary retirement benefits. They have no children. Their existing savings of $300,000 are held in various bank deposits and a hodgepodge of investments. They have surplus income of around $20,000 per year. Here's what happens when they meet with a money-centered adviser (Adviser A) and a life-centered financial planner (Adviser B).

Adviser A

Adviser A conducts a first meeting with Margaret and John. After confirming the reason they have come to see him, Adviser A provides a detailed introduction of himself and his firm, including an explanation of his qualifications and an overview of his advice charges. His questions are mostly focused on identifying the couple's assets available for investment. Adviser A explains his firm's investment philosophy (passive) and why tax efficient investments should continue to be the obvious choice for their investments going forward.

Adviser A explains he needs to assess Margaret and John's attitude toward investment risk and identifies them as medium-risk investors—in part because of the security of their final salary pension benefits. After an additional explanation of his charges and investment philosophy, Adviser A proposes that he put together a financial plan with his recommendations. The couple agrees.

A week later, Adviser A meets Margaret and John again, this time armed with the financial plan he has put together for them. The plan consists of a full breakdown of their current investments, a comparison of past performance and charges for each existing holding, and a detailed recommendation for their new portfolio. His plan for them involves consolidating all their money into a passive investment portfolio on the adviser's wrap platform.

Adviser A explains in further detail the benefits of a passive investment approach, focusing on the low charges. He again explains his adviser charges and asks Margaret and John if they would like to move ahead. Because they have no other plan against which to compare Adviser A's advice, Margaret and John believe they are getting good advice and agree to his recommendations—with the proviso they will limit their initial investment with him to $100,000—one-third of their available assets—to see how Adviser A's recommendations compare against their existing holdings.

Adviser A manages their portfolio efficiently. Over the next 10 years, he recommends that Margaret and John top up their investments just before the end of each tax year, using the same investment philosophy, the same wrap, and with the same adviser charges of 1% per year of their portfolio. A little rebalancing is done annually to ensure the investments stay in line with their risk profile. Adviser A classifies Margaret and John as good clients and is on course to building his firm's assets under management (AUM) by around $400,000 over the next decade, thanks to them.

Adviser B

In his first meeting with Margaret and John, Adviser B does not talk about himself, his firm, his qualifications, his investment philosophy, or charges. Instead, he lets Margaret and John know how grateful he is for the opportunity to meet and explains that, while he has been of great benefit to the person who referred them to him, he cannot guarantee at this stage he will be able to be of benefit to them.

Adviser B explains that he works very differently compared to most advisers. His philosophy is that, until he knows about a client and his or her life, he has no right to talk about their money, much less tell them what to do with it.

The purpose of this first meeting is to find out more about them: where they are in their lives (their current situation), how they got to where they are (their backstory and history), and understand where they are trying to get to in the future (their objectives). Adviser B explains that he will be asking them various questions about the sort of lifestyle they enjoy now and what their future lifestyle might look like.

He explains that during their meeting Margaret and John will also get to learn a little about him and how he operates, so they will be in a position to decide whether they feel comfortable moving ahead. Knowing they can walk away, Margaret and John agree.

Adviser B explains he will be using a confidential financial planning questionnaire so they can make the best use of their time together. He reassures them that, if they do not wish to go any further at the end of the meeting, he will hand them the questionnaire so they can keep (or destroy) it. They agree, again feeling no pressure.

Adviser B now has permission to ask Margaret and John the questions he believes are necessary to best serve their needs. Unlike Adviser A, these questions are not about Margaret and John's *money*. Instead, they are focused on Margaret and John as individuals: their lives, work, hobbies, and interests. What do they want more of? What do they want less of? What do they like? What do they dislike? What sort of life do they enjoy? What do they want to do during the time they have left on earth?

Margaret and John are amazed there is no talk of financial products or investments. It is all about them. They relax and tell Adviser B everything he needs to know. While talking about what they want less of, they explain how stressed they are at work, how they both hate their jobs and cannot wait to retire—an event that was still several years away. They talk about their home and the possibility of downsizing.

Because of the interest Adviser B expressed in Margaret and John as individuals instead of AUM, they end up disclosing all their assets, including a forthcoming inheritance that Margaret will be receiving. They had not shared the same level of information with Adviser A.

Using a short but engaging presentation, Adviser B then explains his *life-centered financial planning* service: how it works, how it helps them see where they are heading financially, and most importantly, whether they are on course to run out of money or die with too much.

Adviser B explains he would like to prepare a comprehensive financial plan. He explains that there will be a fee for this but also explains that he is happy to provide a guarantee: if they do not feel they have benefited in any way, and do not find his plan useful, they do not have to pay the fee.

There is a condition, however. In order to prepare his recommendations for Margaret and John, they will need to complete Adviser B's comprehensive expenditure questionnaire to help him identify the costs of their current and desired future lifestyle. Margaret and John agree.

Over the next two weeks, Adviser B and his paraplanner prepare a comprehensive financial plan using the information Margaret and John provided. Their next meeting with Adviser B is focused on their lives and financial future—there is no discussion of specific investments or products. Adviser B graphically shows them how they are on course to go to their grave with way too much money if they wait to retire until each reaches 66 years of age. Remember, they have no children, but they do have several causes they would like to support.

He shows them an alternative scenario, using conservative assumptions. In this scenario, they can comfortably retire now—seven years early—without fear of running out of money. They currently have a lifestyle they enjoy that also happens to be quite low cost, hence their surplus income. The even better news is that the alternative scenario can include more expenditure on travel and hobbies over the next decade, as well as supporting those causes close to their hearts.

Margaret and John are amazed with the clarity and peace of mind they feel after meeting with Adviser B—the entire focus has been on helping them get the best life possible with the money they have. They can now look forward to an early exit from their stressful jobs.

Margaret and John both understand all their assets need to be aligned and working to achieve the objectives of Adviser B's plan. Without hesitation they agree to invest all their money and future inflows, such as Margaret's inheritance and the proceeds from downsizing their house.

Adviser B has exactly the same platform, tools, and fees as Adviser A, but because his approach is client-focused, not money-focused, he earned the full trust of Margaret and John. Did Adviser A's process fail his clients? We think so. It falls far short of what the financial planning profession can and should be.

This is why life-centered financial planning, as illustrated by Adviser B, is the future of financial planning—it's financial planning focused on clients' lives; their assets play a supporting role. Adviser A may have been a fine and well-qualified professional, but he was using an *inferior process*. As stated previously, good people using inferior processes will always produce inferior results.

Adviser B was using life-centered financial planning to provide Margaret and John with a plan that is all about getting the best life possible with the money they have. That's what we call a *superior* process!

The Journey That Is Life

Imagine your life as a journey that you need to be prepared for in advance. Imagine you were given the opportunity to work with two "travel advisers." The first adviser sits down with you and provides you the costs of fuel, car rental, and public transport in the countries you're traveling to, as well as the costs of lodging, food, and travel insurance—all very useful information. The adviser also offers to prepare a travel budget, promising to try and get you the best price on products and services arranged through her firm.

Now imagine that the second travel adviser offers to do everything the first one offers, but first wants to engage in a discovery conversation with you so she can be better informed on the appropriate logistical arrangements before providing her recommendations. Here's what she asks you:

- What are your destinations?
- What are your objectives for going?

- What are your biggest concerns?
- Who is going with you?
- When the journey is over, what story do you hope to tell?

The first adviser is like the money-centered adviser who is focused on the numbers and making them work. The second adviser is like the life-centered financial planner who is first focused on you—your personal story and motivation—and secondly, on making the numbers work.

Which travel agent would you be most interested in working with to help you manage your journey? Our guess is your own clients would make the same choice!

Next, we're going to discuss how you can bring optimal value to your client relationships and never have them question your worth again.

Chapter 7
Values That Value

The minute you settle for less than you deserve, you get even less than you settled for.

—*Maureen Dowd*

Mitch once interviewed the executive who was responsible for transforming UPS from a package delivery company into a world-class logistics consulting firm. We suspect that there might be an analogy here for those in transit from fees tied to performance, to fees tied to bringing a deeper and more meaningful value to their clients.

This gentleman said that one day he awoke to the realization that UPS was sitting on a goldmine of intellectual property as a result of delivering millions of packages every day to tens of thousands of clients and thousands of outposts through various transportation systems. Who else had such a catbird seat and global knowledge of moving items from point A to point Z?

With this epiphany driving them, they began to package and rebrand themselves as logistics *consultants*. UPS began to offer clients the opportunity to offload all their logistic hassles and management (and by the way, if you like how we manage your logistics, we can deliver the packages as well). This is the intellectual realization and emerging value proposition that transports a firm from a transactional me-too player to a fee-based industry leader. They capitalized on the intellectual property that had always been at their disposal and leveraged it to become exponentially more important in the life and well-being of their clients.

We believe the most sustainable and controllable value proposition available between you and your clients is based primarily on capitalizing on your global knowledge of helping other clients (this is the nucleus of "advice") and building a quality relationship and intimate understanding of what matters most to your clients in relationship to their money. The cross section of this global knowledge and local understanding deserves to be the centerpiece in your value proposition. The processes you employ in wealth management take on a secondary role in service to the value of helping your clients' lives work, and products take on a tertiary role.

Decommoditize

The quotidian value propositions centered on ROI (return on investment)—providing financial planning, asset management, and recommending financial products to achieve returns that we have little control over—are and have undergone rapid commoditization. This is a point we made early in this book. Because of this commoditization, it is becoming increasingly difficult for advisers to differentiate themselves in a crowded, "me too" marketplace or to live up to the unrealistic expectations folded into the ROI approach. So, the first discussion we must have around value is how to distance yourself from the me-too language out there and avoid the whirlpool of commoditization.

What causes commoditization to take place in the first place? *Comparability* is the chief dynamic pulling prices downward and keeping a gravitational weight upon them. When most consumers purchase an item or service, they do comparative shopping. If it's a house, you go online and search for comparable properties. The same can be said when shopping for a car or a household appliance.

When Mitch speaks in front of a group of financial advisers, he often asks them, "How many of you are bothered by a local competitor who claims to do exactly what you do but doesn't do it nearly as well?" Almost every hand goes up. His question to those with uplifted hands and miffed visages is, "And whose problem is that?

If you don't want to be compared to other advisers, stop sounding like them."

If a prospective client sits and listens to your description of services rendered—with the same nomenclature as the pitch they just heard down the street—we cannot fault them for thinking, "Well, that sounds the same to me, so I'll just go with the one with the lower price." However, if you sound unique and deliver the type of client experience they've never encountered before, they have nothing with which to compare you and begin mentally scaling down the value of your services.

A psycho-emotive key to developing a value proposition that will only appreciate over time and not be subjected to the forces of depreciation is: deliver on value that is *felt but not measurable*. Although not a perfect analogy, we think this example is a good one—it was given to Mitch by a professional scout when he asked what the scout was looking for in a prospective player: "The same thing everyone else is looking for: speed, strength, and agility. But there is one other component they must have, or we will not risk millions of dollars and a first-round draft choice on them—they must have *coachability*."

Coachability is important, but how do you measure it? The bottom line is that coachability is a value that is observable and felt, but there's no objective way to measure it. Like work ethic or esprit de corps, these traits are observable and felt but there is no standardized method for measurement. Because speed, strength, and agility are easy to measure, they are seen as commodities (in the scouting community) that lack value without the underlying *intangible values*.

Intangible value is what will sustain your value as a life-centered financial planner. Prospects and clients look for certain values to be present in their financial lives and are willing to pay a premium to see those values implemented.

If any of the following statements describe you, you are at risk:

- You need to constantly (quarterly/annually) prove your worth.
- You are blamed for events and forces beyond your control.

- You are perpetually compared to competitors and indexes.
- You are wrong in your predictions.
- You have to cope with clients who hold back information and assets.
- You have too many clients.
- You do not have enough time in your day to balance personal and professional commitments.

What this list illustrates is the inevitable failure of poorly founded value propositions. When we start with the wrong hub in our proposition, we should not be surprised when the entire wheel becomes unbalanced. What we need in order to retain clients and sustain success is what Mitch likes to call a *val-YOU proposition*—or simply defined as "our business proposition is good for you." If it's not good for you, then it's not good for your clients over time because you'll burn out. And if it's not good for you, it's not good for the companies you're affiliated with because the level of your success will be unsustainable. This is the pattern ultimately leading to what Mitch likes to refer to as "practicide"—building a business designed to kill you over time.

We've seen more than our share of companies out there who claim to want to serve clients well but exert absurd levels of pressure on production and assets under management (AUM)—and consequently burn out valid talent and people with the right stuff. Making promises we can't keep is an important discussion for the future of this profession. Your clients are looking for a value proposition: a promise from you to the client.

Core Values

If your goal is to bring value that cannot be commoditized, you need to understand the intangible values your clients want and need in their financial lives that only life-centered financial advisers can deliver. The six core values of the adviser/client relationship in the life-centered financial planning model are as follows:

Organization: We will help bring order to your financial life.
Accountability: We will help you follow through on your financial commitments.
Objectivity: We will provide insight from the outside to help you avoid emotionally driven decisions in important money matters.
Proactivity: We will help you anticipate the key transitions in your life so that you will be financially prepared for them.
Education: We will explore the specific knowledge you will need to succeed in your situation.
Partnership: We will work with you to help you achieve the best life possible.

Let's examine these core values one by one—bearing in mind that all of them are observable and felt by the client but are not measurable and therefore outside the scope of commoditization. You know you're delivering immeasurable value when the recipient uses superlatives to describe the impact: incredible, invaluable, and priceless are examples of what you want to hear.

Organization: *We will help bring order to your financial life.*

Mitch once met a financial planner that opened her conversation with prospects by talking about an old cable television show she used to watch called *Clean Sweep*. On the show, organization coaches would go into disheveled homes and help bring order. She would tell the potential client, "They would take *everything* out of the house and put it into one of three piles: (1) keep; (2) get rid of; and (3) let's talk. This is how I start with my clients. We go into your financial house and put everything you have into one of those three piles."

Not only was this a brilliant metaphor but an excellent articulation of the visceral value of working with this planner. Having order in our financial lives is a need felt by almost everyone—and the result of achieving that order is *calmness*. How hard is it to value calmness in our financial lives? It's felt but not measurable.

Accountability: We will help you follow through on your financial commitments.

Personal and executive coaching is a billion-dollar business and growing. There are over 50,000 certified coaches across the globe. There are thousands more who haven't pursued certification and recognition by any coaching organization. What's driving this?

In short, people's desire for accountability.

If I hire a personal trainer, I don't pay them $85/hour to stand over me at a weight-lifting station and count to 12. I hire them to hold me accountable to show up and commit to staying in shape. As an adviser, think of yourself as your client's fiscal trainer.

One observation about successful people is that they have reached their level of success as a result of having laser vision—they are focused on one thing and do it very well. The shadow side of these successful people is that there are many matters in their lives that are neglected, undone, or half-baked. This is where the need for accountability comes in—they know they need it and are willing to pay for it.

We like to describe the accountability a fiscal coach brings as "holding your feet to the fire of your stated best intentions."

Objectivity: We will provide insight from the outside to help you avoid emotionally driven decisions in important money matters.

True advisers don't tell people what they want to hear; they tell them what they *need* to hear. If we hire an attorney at $400/hour to advise us, we don't want them calibrating their advice for our itching ears—we want to hear the truths and perspectives that we need to know. This is something that sales-oriented advisers can't do. They are afraid of losing the sale, so they often say what a client wants to hear, thereby doing that client a disservice.

If I have a conflict of interest, then I can't deliver advice objectively. If I'm worried about AUM, I might tacitly avoid encouraging spending that might benefit my client's well-being. Objectivity is about giving a point of reference that is not prejudiced by my particular need or want but only by what is best for my client. This is the heart and soul of the fiduciary standard.

Proactivity: We will help you anticipate the key transitions in your life so that you will be financially prepared for them.

Earlier, we mentioned the economic law of life that *money goes into motion when life goes in transition.* The sales forces in the financial services realm would like to pretend that there are basically three life transitions: child going to college, retirement, and death—the lion's share of products they proffer are tied to those three transitions. Mitch has spent 20 years researching life transitions and has discovered over 60 life transitions from the cradle to grave—and they all have financial implications tied to them. In other words, the potential to ameliorate or harm our financial status is present in all transitions in life, to varying degrees. Obviously, a divorce has greater implications than, say, becoming an empty nester, but there are always financial considerations we need to understand to navigate through successfully.

In Chapter 13, we discuss how to begin and continue the axiomatic life transitions dialogue with your clientele. Not only does it bring a deep personalization to the planning process, it obviates the financial risk that could lead to your client's fiscal undoing.

Education: We will explore the specific knowledge you will need to succeed in your situation.

We've come to the conclusion that the best life-centered financial planners are teachers or instructors at heart. They don't try to embellish their value by leaving clients in the dark; instead, they bolster their value by bringing clients into the light. Clients will always be appreciative of advisers who increase their understanding around key financial issues.

While we believe traditional financial literacy is important, the kind of education we're talking about is behavioral and emotional in nature. It is educating the limbic part of your client's brain on how they can let emotions get in the way of good financial decision-making.

True advisers have an obligation to do their best to keep clients from sabotaging their own situations. Becoming versed in the basics of behavioral finance is the beginning. Having the courage to confront the issues in the first place is fundamental to delivering this educational value in your practice.

Partnership: We will work with you to help you achieve the best life possible.

You cannot help the clients who will not help themselves. You're in the boat rowing, but you should not be rowing alone. Successful partnerships hinge on proper expectations first and delivering on those expectations secondly.

What are your client's expectations of you? Have you ever asked? A financial planning veteran once told Mitch that at the end of every prospect meeting he would pull out a legal pad and ask, "If we were to work together, what would you expect from me as an adviser?" He said he had learned that it was much easier to appoint than it was to disappoint, and that he wanted to know upfront what a client's expectations were so he could truthfully answer them or decline the opportunity. If a prospect said, "I expect 12% returns annually," John would simply drop his pen and say, "I'm sorry I can't deliver on that expectation. I know someone down the street who will tell you he can if that's what you must have."

Conversely, you have every right to let clients know what your expectations are *of them*. Have you ever thought of prefacing your investment policy statements with an investment philosophy statement? In this statement you could define what clients could expect from you and what you expect from them. Partnerships work when you know what to expect from each other.

Making the Leap

Each quantum leap in the financial services sector has introduced new disciplines into the financial discussion. In the leap forward from sales transactions to asset management and asset allocation, risk-profiling tools were introduced. In the leap forward from asset management to financial planning, probability analysis, goals inquiry, and more comprehensive discovery tools were introduced into the discussion. In the leap forward into life-centered financial planning, life-transition tracking tools, financial satisfaction, and fiscal philosophy and behavioral tools have been (and continue to be) developed to help clients merge their money and lives.

The approaches and the processes promoted in the past are no longer enough to convince clients to entrust their hard-earned and easily evaporating assets to advisers and planners who cannot assure them the future will be any better. Clients are looking for professionals who will keep the promises they make—and the profession is seeking a value proposition it can fulfill. The answer is no longer based on predicting the markets, guaranteeing returns, or outpacing competing asset managers, but rather on building a financial practice focused on the life and well-being of *the client*. Helping them organize, holding them accountable, telling the truth, helping them to be proactive, educating them on positive financial behaviors and being their partner... now these are all promises you can keep, year in and year out.

Chapter 8
Soft Skills Are Really the Hard Stuff

The greatest obstacle to discoveries is not ignorance—it is the illusion of knowledge.

—Daniel Boorstin

For years we've heard the mocking and subtly pejorative terms bandied about at financial conventions about "soft skills," "squishy questions," and more. This sort of parlance had more to do with the comfort zones of the utterers than they did about the relevance of the competencies being discussed. The fact of the matter is that there are still planners out there that think that what matters most are the facts. But we have discovered, as was poignantly captured by industry consultant Scott West, "If you stick to the facts, the facts don't stick," and "The soft skills are the harder stuff."

Mitch, who lives in Rochester, Minnesota—home of the world-renowned Mayo Clinic—says that the transformation of the role and competencies required of advisers today reminds him of the development path of physicians' "bedside manner" in the last decade or two, which was a more hit-or-miss proposition years ago. Some MDs showed up with a more scientific and less personal bearing, while others showed up with a more decidedly relational bearing. But showing up impersonally—armed with scientific reasoning and facts—has become less acceptable as research continues to demonstrate that patients recover better when they know that their doctor cares.[1] Empathy aids the recovery process, and being armed with intelligence is no longer enough if not accompanied by emotional intelligence.

The same can be said for the role of the adviser. Being armed with the facts, intelligent explanations of how markets and investments work, proficiency in all monetary mechanics, and planning proficiencies no longer suffice if not delivered empathically.

In the last 30 years we have seen a proliferation of universities with programs in personal financial planning with a growing emphasis on *personal*. Texas Tech University was 1 of 20 programs registered by the CFP board in 1987. They also registered a PhD program in 2000 that has sent out 55 professors to date to teach at other institutes of higher learning. Today there are over 225 schools with personal finance or financial planning programs. These programs are teaching much more than basic planning competencies. They are teaching counseling and coaching, financial psychology, behavioral finance, and many other aspects that will prepare planners of the future to be more holistically equipped. What skill sets will be necessary to meet the future?

Take a look at the curricula that are being taught in the personal finance or financial planning departments, and you'll see topics like improving listening skills, understanding personality and temperaments, coaching and counseling competencies, understanding money scripts, dealing with grief and loss, managing difficult conversations, dealing with reluctant client behavior, and uncovering psychological biases (the list goes on and on). The focus is clearly shifting toward managing human tendencies and thinking, as much as it is the managing of a client's assets and financial plans.

We asked Sarah Asebedo, PhD, CFP, from Texas Tech University, "What do you see as the key competencies that the adviser of the future must develop?" Her answer was,

The adviser of the future (really the adviser of today) must have therapeutic skills (e.g., empathy, listening, behavioral intervention techniques, conflict management) that help the adviser connect the client's underlying "human" characteristics (e.g., values, biases, personality, social relationships, etc.) to their money. They will also need to have the ability to execute these skills in a digital environment.

Dr. Asebedo, who teaches a course on counseling and coaching skills that is part of a certificate program for life-centered financial planning, also mentioned that they are training not only traditional students but many practicing advisers through distance learning. These advisers in the life-centered financial planning class have commented that the skills they learned have helped them bring on new clients and connect with existing clients in a more meaningful way.

This skill set discussion is, first and foremost, about comportment before it's about content, and about posture before it's about postulation. It's about how we show up, not about how we show off. We remember the words of financial philosopher Jacob Needleman when asked after the Great Recession what clients needed most after seeing their assets cut in half: "They need to know that they've been heard."

Before we move into the next chapter on questions, we want to place the spotlight on personal comportment rather than content; on our ability to show up in a conversation and let people know they've been heard; and to gain ground in the most important dynamics in forging relationships—empathy and resonance.

Yes, it is important to have a working knowledge of behavioral finance and to be able to translate it into simplified language. Yes, you'll want to continue sharpening your counseling and coaching skill sets, as well as your biographical abilities with clients. Any study you choose to pursue on how humans think and behave will raise both your awareness and competence relationally with clients. Learn all you can about the people business—ultimately, this is what will pay the bills.

The Self-Centered Self-Delusion

Your clients live in their own world. You live in yours. Is it possible to tune into clients well enough in conversation to break out of the gravitational pull of your planet and make a permanent landing on theirs? Only if you have a good understanding of the nature of the gravitational pull of your own planet and have the empathetic willpower to launch through the atmosphere that keeps you hinged to your own concerns.

We remember years ago reading about a study conducted on the communications skills of investment advisers. The findings, if nothing else, confirmed how easy it is to overestimate one's own level of empathy. The gist of what the researchers found, in a nutshell, was that the vast majority of advisers thought that their clients were content with their communication skills, but the majority of clients stated that their adviser was falling short of their expectations in communication. Such a disparity in perception lies at the root of human nature's inclination to assume "things are fine" without actually surveying the contentment on the side of the recipient.

In order for client relationships to progress, your client must be much more impressed with your listening skills than they are with your presentation skills. It's possible to be the greatest presenter in the room and yet still be the worst communicator. Don't we all know someone who fits this description? Isn't this person sometimes you or us?

A paper presented by Professors S. Clay Willmington and Milda M. Steinbrecher from the University of Wisconsin-Oshkosh found that there are four major factors (within ourselves) interfering with effective listening, especially in any setting where a service is sold.[2] These are the gravitational forces and instincts that keep us trying to pull people toward our planet instead of making a successful landing on theirs. For the sake of recall, we have formed the following acronym (SEED) to identify the four factors that keep us from really tuning in. Think of them as *the seeds of client discontent*:

S – Self-Focus: We are so concerned with our own agenda and pushing that agenda that we struggle to tune into the speaker.

E – Egocentricity: At times we simply like to hear the sound of our own voice, and our favorite topics are what we have done, what we think, and how successful we have been. Egocentricity also places more emphasis on being witty, clever, and smart than actually hearing the other party.

E – Experiential Superiority: When a client is talking, we start thinking, "I've heard this story before" (or something very close to this) and find it difficult to resist the impulse to jump in and reveal that we "already know where this is going" or to offer input on the assumed objective of what they are saying.

D – Defensiveness: If someone doesn't agree with our advice or ideas, the first impulse is to become emotionally agitated and defend our view and opinion. This builds a wall between us and hobbles our ability to listen.

"He just doesn't listen!" we heard a woman say as she explained why she had just changed 401(k) vendors for her company. "I would look this guy in the eye and tell him what I wanted and needed, and he would just continue to push his own agenda. Obviously, this was not about us for him, so we switched. And technically, he probably had a slightly better product. But I can't deal with the lack of understanding anymore."

It would hardly be possible to quantify how many relationships are lost by people with poor listening skills, but we're confident the monetary loss would be in the billions. As individuals, we must ask ourselves how much a lack of listening might be costing our business. Is it possible that some of our clients—ones we assume are satisfied with the way we communicate—would say they are not so satisfied? The safest premise we can operate from is this: "I can always do a better job of listening." It's better to adopt this attitude, because it will safeguard us from smugness, arrogance, and the sort of hubris that causes important relationships to fail.

Those who possess excellent inquiry skills are usually curious and genuinely interested in others by nature. Yet they have also learned that these skills must be purposefully developed with practice and good habits.

The Empathy Report Card

If your clients were to fill out a listening skills report on you (Figure 8.1), how well do you think you would score?

The reality is that clients and prospects won't give us this sort of report card—they will just go elsewhere! Therefore, we must simply develop a mindfulness and awareness about superior listening skills. If you want to be pulled into the same orbit as your clients, you'll need to pay closer attention when they talk and to how tuned in your responses are to the actual content of what they are saying. Don't expect clients to follow your lead simply because of your erudition and brilliance. We may be initially attracted to shooting stars ... but don't follow them for long.

The following words by Søren Kierkegaard, the famed Danish philosopher, theologian, and social critic, may be some of the most

The Empathy Scorecard

LISTENING SKILL	LISTENING GRADE				
1. The adviser gives me their undivided attention when I am talking.	A ☐	B ☐	C ☐	D ☐	F ☐
2. The adviser is tuned into me rather than thinking of their own response.	A ☐	B ☐	C ☐	D ☐	F ☐
3. The adviser answers in a way that reflects my major concerns.	A ☐	B ☐	C ☐	D ☐	F ☐
4. The adviser keeps conversation polarized on my needs, issues, and concerns.	A ☐	B ☐	C ☐	D ☐	F ☐
5. The adviser gives a summary of what I have told them and of their intended response.	A ☐	B ☐	C ☐	D ☐	F ☐

Figure 8.1 The empathy scorecard.
SOURCE: Mitch Anthony.

incisive and penetrating thoughts ever penned on the posture our ego must assume if we are to truly help people make progress:

> If one is truly to succeed in leading a person to a specific place, one must first and foremost take care to find him where he is and begin there.
>
> This is the secret in the entire art of helping.
>
> Anyone who cannot do this is himself under a delusion if he thinks he is able to help someone else. In order to truly help someone else, I must understand more than he—but certainly first and foremost understand what he understands.
>
> If I do not do that, then my greater understanding does not help him at all. If I nevertheless want to assert my greater understanding, then it is because I am vain or proud, then basically instead of benefiting him I really want to be admired by him.
>
> But all true helping begins with a humbling.
>
> The helper must first humble himself under the person he wants to help and thereby understand that to help is not to dominate but to serve, that to help is not to be the most dominating but the most patient, that to help is a willingness for the time being to put up with being in the wrong and not understanding what the other understands.[3]

Open ears can help train a restless tongue. A humbleness of heart and a true desire to understand the person we seek to help is the posture required to open our ears to their full capacity. Our relational capacity will never exceed our listening capacity. This is the inviolable law of human connectivity. This is how to fight the gravitational forces that make us want to pull everyone's attention back to ourselves. This is how empathy is forged and how empathic personalities develop.

"I Feel You, Man"

We define resonance as hearing that which echoes our own story or experience. We feel a sense of resonance with those whose account of life reminds us of the lessons we have learned. We feel a connection to them because of this mutual understanding. Resonance should be our primary aim in any conversation.

We would all do well to occasionally inspect our communication, our content, and introspect on the question, "What is my goal here?" Is it to convince, to persuade, to document, to establish proficiency and efficacy? If these are our primary goals in communication, we are aiming too low. We would submit the idea that the highest value and most lasting result that can come from a dialogue is resonance. We get this word from a Latin term that means "to echo." Whether we sit down in a meaningful dialogue with one or two, or stand up and speak to 100 or 200, we want to know that the things we are saying are echoing with our audiences.

Our stories are never an even tale. We've all contributed to the ebbing trials as much or more than we have to the rising tides. As much as we may love to hear about "rules of success," we can all, more intimately, relate to stumbling our way to victories that may come. True resonance is about hitting these chords of human fallibility in the soul of our audience. Think of the songs that resonate with you in a deep way and ask yourself, "Why?" "Why that song?" "Why those words?" It is most likely because those words echo with your own experience.

Mitch remembers years ago receiving a call from a principal of a large urban high school where he was scheduled to speak. The principal nervously inquired about the content of his talk. Mitch described the talk as being about how to deal with mockery and humiliation as a result of being harassed over a crooked eye in his school years, and loss and grief over losing a best friend to a drowning accident brought on by some poor choices.

"Oh, thank goodness," the principal replied. "We don't need to hear from anymore #%$^%& astronauts!" He wanted a talk that would resonate with the real-life experiences and struggles of adolescence; not a talk about how they too, could go to the moon.

Pathways to Resonance

If we reflect on conversations we have greatly enjoyed, we'll realize that there are some common threads that led to us feeling resonance and that ignited our appreciation of that person. Let's take a look under the hood of resonance and look at the pathways that lead to resonance, the roadblocks that prevent it, and finally, examine its articulation. Following are the dynamics in discourse we have observed that seem to stir resonance in a dialogue. The dialogue dynamics are followed by the emotion triggered within the party we are conversing with. The audience's thought or emotional impact follows in parentheses:

1. Speaking out loud the heretofore tacit truth about a matter.
    ("I've always thought that but didn't know how to say it.")
2. Articulating frailty, fallibility, and vulnerability.
    ("I was fooled." "I was wrong." "I wasn't thinking.")
3. Baring your soul in a matter.
    ("I wish I could be that honest.")
4. Asking the elephant-in-the-room question.
    ("I need to deal with this.")
5. Calling out hypocrisy and pretense.
    ("No kidding.")
6. Humbly admitting a lack of expertise.
    ("It's easy to listen to someone who's not full of themselves.")
7. Expressing gratitude.
    ("Everybody needs help along the way.")
    NOTE: *Humility and gratitude could be called the two universally embraced languages of resonance.*
8. Humor at your own expense.
    ("It's fun to listen to people who can laugh at themselves.")
9. Using a story or illustration.
    ("Personal truth is best revealed in an analogy, parable, or story.")

Roadblocks to Resonance

If we reflect on conversations that we have not enjoyed, we'll realize there are also some common threads that led to us feeling a lack of resonance and ignited our unappreciation of the person. Just as we can incorporate a manner of speaking that fosters resonance, we can also unwittingly slip into ego-driven, lusting-for-admiration, approval-seeking slips of the lips that dissuade our audience from trusting us too nearly or too dearly. These are some of the leading roadblocks to resonance we've noted in dialogue:

1. Playing the expert.
    (Error detector goes on high alert.)
2. Telling stories where the punchline is that you're somehow the hero ... again.
    ("Well, if you don't say so yourself. Apparently, a legend in his own mind.")
3. Providing too much information; not enough story.
    ("You're boring us to death.")
4. Using hackneyed clichés and platitudes/echoes of other people's material.
    ("Blah, blah, blah ... What do you actually think?")
5. Advertised vanity.
    ("Sell me on being interested not on being interesting.")
6. A self-satisfied semblance and expression.
    ("So, you're that much smarter than me?")
7. Grandiose build-up.
    (Too much showmanship to be trusted.)
8. Running down the competition.
    ("Wonder what he'll say about me behind my back?")
9. Using judgmental tones and didactic approach.
    ("Can't be easy being Mr. Wonderful.")

If we're succeeding in hitting home with clients and prospects, we'll hear the affirmations of that resonance in the form of expressions such as:

"I hear you."

"That's the truth."

"That's been my experience.

"Touché!"

"That's how it is."

We would like to add here that the greatest level of resonance always comes from a love of the truth superseding the love of approval. This applies to an audience of one or an audience of many. It's also interesting to note that many an expert, influencer, and adviser violate the paths to resonance with great frequency and stumble into the roadblocks equally as often. What is required is awareness of ourselves, vigilance regarding our comportment in conversation, and the unwavering commitment to sieve out what is best for our client. This alignment of heart, emotions, and speech will not fail in delivering a sense of security and faith to our clients.

You Gotta Serve Somebody

Developing transcendent human-to-human capabilities. Becoming a better listener. Evoking empathy in conversation. Resonating with others' stories. Counseling and coaching clients. Understanding the role of emotion in financial behavior. Hearing and respecting others' experiences and stories. What does it all add up to? Something quite simple—that the so-called soft skills are the harder stuff, but they do carry the day.

As you make these skills your central focus, you begin realizing that the business models the industry and profession espouse were not designed with these skill sets in mind. The heretofore models were designed with the idea of gathering assets, managing assets, and retaining assets with just enough relational effort on the periphery to keep it friendly. When you turn that model inside out and put the person first, instead of their assets, then it makes perfect sense to optimize our capacity for connecting with people. The assets will come. When we figure out the kind of person we need to show up as, the opportunities will spell themselves out to us, because we will know what type of client resonates with us. When we treat clients the best we possibly can, the best possible clients just seem to show up.

It is certainly true that we cannot take on as clients every person we like who lacks assets or the ability to pay our fees, as we would inevitably go out of business. But with asset minimums and net worth thresholds, we could just as easily miss wonderful opportunities for serving some remarkable clients. There's got to be some moral latitude and balance in how we determine whom we can and will not serve.

A financial planner in Pennsylvania told us the story of a man who came to him deeply in debt and with negligible assets; in fact, he was upside down in net worth. He told the planner he needed help to plan his way out of his situation. The planner said that he had always left room in his month for pro bono or lower-priced planning work—especially where he sensed that the client had genuine aspirations. He agreed to develop a plan for this fellow, and the man stuck to the plan. The man was a software engineer working with a tech start-up. Five years later, the man's company was sold, and he was rewarded with a $75 million payday (I'm sure you can guess whom he entrusted assets with). The adviser told us, "I had no idea anything like that would happen; I just wanted to see him turn his situation around."

That is the kind of planner everyone in the world wants to work with.

Keep the "who" straight, and the "what" will come. Conversely, if you give the "what" precedence, be careful of "who" you might become. In an industry that places great meaning on the "what," and pressures you to do so as well, it might be best to follow the maxim of Horton the Elephant: "A person's a person, no matter how small."

Notes

1. Stephanie Lecci and Mitch Teich, "How Your Doctor Feels about You Could Affect Your Care." WUWM: December 3, 2013. https://www
.wuwm.com/post/how-your-doctor-feels-about-you-could-
affect-your-care#stream/0.

2. S. Clay Willmington and Milda M. Steinbrecher, "Assessing Listening in the Basic Course: The University of Wisconsin-Oshkosh Listening Test." Presented at the 1993 Joint Convention of the Central States Communication Association and the Southern Speech Communication Association, Lexington, KY. April 1993. https://eric.ed.gov/?id=ED360662

3. Søren Kierkegaard, *The Essential Kierkegaard*, eds. Howard V. Hong and Edna H. Hong (Princeton, NJ: Princeton University Press, 2000).

Chapter 9
Answers Get Questioned, Questions Get Answered

Always the beautiful answer who asks a more beautiful question.
—E. E. Cummings

Today we live in a messaging culture where messages get sent more effectively than they are often received. Voice messaging, text messaging, posting on Facebook, Twitter, Instagram, and other social media are all forms of this modern messaging. This messaging mentality and modality can easily creep into our face-to-face conversations if we are not aware of the potential for it to happen.

It's helpful to understand the fundamental difference between a *monologue* and a *dialogue*. They are universes apart and are not interchangeable in nature. We'll explain. These terms come from the Greek word *dialogos*; the "logos" is concerned with the meaning being communicated in the conversation.

Monologos

The Greek root word *monologos* translates to "speaking alone," as in *monologue*: one person doing all the talking. According to the definition at vocabulary.com, a monologue is "a speech delivered

91

by one person, or a long one-sided conversation that makes you want to pull your hair out from boredom."

Monologues are fine if we're watching a stage show like *Waiting for Godot* but rarely are as entertaining in the real world where people are calculating how to get out from under the blowhard or self-absorbed person doing all the talking.

Another note of importance here is that in studying sales presentations, one cannot help but note that they are almost always built on the chassis of a monologue. The presentation usually starts by asking a cliché question that the inquirer either knows the answer to or can predict the answer to, so that they can continue with their previously intended monologue. Do you remember a time where someone asked you a "set up" question and then went full speed ahead with their premeditated pitch? It was rather insulting, wasn't it? Our brains have an intuitive antenna for such interlocutionary disingenuousness.

This is not true in the case of the *dialogue*—a conversation that typically starts with a question that one could not predict the answer to and is being asked out of genuine curiosity.

Dialogos

While monologists seek to assert their solo meaning, dialogists seek to *merge meaning* with the other party in the dialogue. The act of dialogue is focused on inquiring to the point of understanding and bringing the understanding to the level of being able to explain the other party's point of view, as well as the reason they arrived at that perspective. In other words, you're now walking in their shoes. The ultimate end of a dialogue then is to create a shared sense of meaning.

According to the William C. Friday Fellowship for Human Relations,[1] the following guidelines lead to effective dialogues:

1. *Listen actively and without judgment.* Listen intently to what is said and try to pick up on the feelings being expressed under the words (read between the lines). Listen to yourself as well as

others. Affirm the rights of others to hold their perspectives by listening intently and avoid prepping your response when listening to another. Be aware of and set aside your judgments.

2. *Speak from the "I" position.* It is very common to use *you* instead of *I*. As you pay attention to this, you will see how much more powerful using "I" statements will be—speaking only for yourself, not for the whole community, not for the person sitting next to you.

3. *Accept messiness and practice nonclosure.* Stay comfortable even if the conversation feels a little messy and realize that not all complex issues always get resolved in one dialogue. You don't have to have your statements worked out before you start talking or have any answers—your perspectives and thoughts are enough. Accept that both yourself and others are disorganized in thought and share as openly as possible. Dialogue is more like a spontaneous party dance than a rehearsed ballroom routine.

4. *Focus on your learning.* Your intention is to learn from others, to expand your view and understanding—not to evaluate the other or to determine who has the "best" view. Ask questions for clarification and exercise genuine curiosity.

5. *Maintain confidentiality.* We must agree that nothing that is said here is shared elsewhere and that nothing that is shared is taken out of context, in any way. Also remember that when you see each other outside of this context, respect that people may or may not want to discuss issues raised here after they leave.

6. *Practice both/and thinking.* Look for ways in which ideas fit together and avoid setting up an either/or process or a competition between ideas. One does not have to be false to make the other true. It is quite possible that both are true. Being able to accept that two seemingly contradictory views of the world could both be true is challenging but is regarded by many as a hallmark of real intelligence.

7. *Practice inquiry and discovery versus perfection.* We are engaged in a process of inquiry and discovery together. Our task is to

engage authentically in an ongoing journey and always remember to be conscious of allowing discovery to emerge for yourself and others through an inquiring approach.

Really Smart People

The way some financial professionals comport themselves in an introductory meeting, you would guess that the goal is to *be interesting* instead of *being interested* in the person in front of them. Competence in financial matters should be a baseline, but very few prospective clients are impressed by those who work too hard at being impressive.

If your chief goal is to promenade your system, your process, or your vast knowledge of how things work, you will always run the risk of running afoul of one the most basic truths of human interaction—the invisible sign that hangs around every neck—"Help me feel important." Your system, process, and knowledge do matter, but not if the seeds of them are being sown in unreceptive soil.

Savvy communicators are aware of the annoyances and irritations that can easily enter a conversation. Scott McDowell, author of *The New Managers Handbook*,[2] offers the five following examples of how we can easily turn off an audience of one or many:

1. *Acting Like a Sage.* An adviser is inherently in a position of authority, and it's easy to let that power get in the way. Before the thought or conversation is complete, you already think you know the answer. This type of barrier is a prejudgment. Rather than having all the answers, it is your job to coax the answers to the surface.

2. *Hasty Problem Solving.* Solving a problem too early in the process of conversation can cause an emotional barrier between the adviser and his or her audience that is difficult to reverse. Instead of prematurely attempting to solve a client's problem, give yourself the opportunity to fully understand and learn from the discussion.

3. *Competitive Listening.* This is a problem area where the natural leader assumes control of the conversation by interrupting. A competitive interruption occurs in order to challenge an assumption, provoke a response, influence the conversation, or impress.

4. *Reacting to Red Flag Words.* Quickly reacting to red flag language—anything that can be deemed inflammatory or emotionally difficult—can derail a conversation and short-circuit a learning opportunity. The best path is to be unbiased, let the moment occur, and respond appropriately rather than in an emotionally infused retort.

5. *Obvious Physical Distractions.* Clearing the decks of all distraction should be the first step in an important one-on-one conversation. That means curtailing access to the internet, powering down the device, and closing the door to the office. All physical distractions have the potential to divert from a meaningful dialogue.

The bottom line on *really* smart people is that they don't feel the need to play the guru, the expert, the end-all to all conversations. They are comfortable drawing answers out of the people in the dialogue, educing their stories and perspectives in the quest for resonant insight and understanding. They are in the proper posture and frame of mind to engage in true discovery: for them, great questions are the tools skillfully wielded in the greater quest.

Meaningful Questions

The questions we ask should address the quest—or what matters most to the client. Chasing a number is not what matters most. What matters most is taking care of those they love, achieving the life they imagine, and leaving an honorable legacy in this world. These are true quests. Before we offer some time-tested dialogue starters, we want to first address the issue of client comfort in a conversation.

Here are some ground rules to abide by if we hope to take dialogue to a deeper level:

- Don't dive deep out of the blue.
- Establish context for what you're going to be asking.
- Anchor the story; link the story you hear to the service you'll be delivering.

Don't Dive Deep Out of the Blue

There are many advocates for deeper lines of questioning in the financial advice world. We take the point of view that an adviser should enter the depth of conversation one layer at a time so as not to blindside clients with questions that to them seem an ill fit for conversing with a financial professional. If you were to go to your dentist, and she opened the conversation in the chair with, "Tell me about your most traumatic childhood memory," you might be wondering, "Why are *you* asking me *that*?"

Is it fair to think that financial services clients could be equally flummoxed if asked a question that seems far afield to what they were expecting when they entered the meeting? Mitch talked to one company that had bought into a system of repeating a rather deep question over and over until their advisers were satisfied that they had reached the bottom of their client's hopes in life. This company told Mitch that after a year of using this system, they sent out a survey to their advisers—and 70% of the advisers responded that they were uncomfortable with the line of questioning and felt awkward asking. That awkwardness is palpable to the person being asked. If the questioner is not perfectly comfortable with an inquiry, you can be sure the party on the other side will also be ill at ease.

We go with the theory that advisers are better off scraping the surface before resorting to fracking deep into the earth. Work your way into the deeper ground one step at a time. For example, in the history inquiry the levels of discovery might look like this:

Level 1: Where are you from originally?
Level 2: What was it like growing up there? What did your parents do?

Level 3: What was money like growing up?
Level 4: What is one of your earliest recollections in life around money?

If we attempt to start this conversation at level four, we might sense some immediate hesitance and confusion, thereby squelching the momentum of the dialogue before it goes into full swing. You get the point.

Establish Context for What You're Going to Be Asking

The first thing the right side of our brain wants to know in any conversation is, "Why are you asking this?" There's something in our brains that needs *context* before it feels comfortable moving forward. One of the tools we've developed over the years is *context opening scripts* for the various dialogues between advisers and their clients. These context openers go something like this:

> *Adviser:*   Mr. and Mrs. Client, one of the most important lessons I've learned in my 20 years in this profession is that it's not enough to just know my client's financials, accounts, etc. More important for me is to know your story first, especially your experiences with money and investing and related topics. If you don't mind, I'd love to ask you a few questions along those lines.
> (The adviser then pauses.)
>
> *Client:*   Yes, please, go right ahead.

Note what you've accomplished with this dialogue opener:

- You've noted an important lesson you've learned as an adviser.
- You've established context around *why* you are about to ask what you're going to ask (no surprises now).
- You've indicated your interest in understanding them better (most people are flattered at this).
- You've gained their permission to move forward.

Anchor the Story; Link the Story You Hear to the Service You'll Be Delivering

The most respectful thing to do once we've heard someone's story or perspective is to let them know what we are going to do as a result of our having heard what they just told us. This is the closing part of the dialogue that we refer to as *anchoring*. This is where we make a tangible connection between the story the client told and the planning/advisory service we will provide.

Here's an example: "After hearing your story about how your mother struggled to make ends meet after your father passed away, I would imagine that has always been a concern to you as well. Maybe a good place for us to start our risk management work would be to double-check on all your important insurances to make sure they are what they ought to be."

Here's another example, one in which someone has conveyed a story about a less than desirable experience with a previous adviser: "After hearing about the poor communication and confusing investments you've experienced in the past, I might suggest that we cooperatively lay out a yearly schedule for talking to make sure you are clear on where your money is and your level of risk."

The important thing to leave your clients with is that fact that *they have been heard*. This is what all humans hope for in important conversations. Anchoring ensures that this level of satisfaction is viscerally and rationally met.

Questions for the Quest

And now—what we imagine you were hoping for when you opened up this chapter—here are some really good and interesting questions you can ask your prospects and clients. We've already laid out a few questions for beginning the *history inquiry*, but we'll add them below.

Where are you from originally?
What was it like growing up there? What did your parents do?

How did you get started in this business? What were you doing before?
Tell me about your career path so far.
Tell me about your family.
What was money like growing up?
What would you describe as your best and worst financial experiences so far?
Have you had any experiences with any other financial professionals, good or bad, that would be worth your time to tell me about?

We strongly suggest adding this question toward the end of your history inquiry with clients. It will give you a clear idea of their post-traumatic advice experiences as well as their expectations of you going forward.

What is one of your earliest recollections in life around money?

The answers to this question are fun to explore with the follow-up question, "Why do you suppose your mind sent that recollection?" There's a reason the recollection was stored away in the memory bank—and the lesson that comes with it is usually something of considerable significance regarding money.

Has anything happened so far in your life that you would describe as a defining moment?

If the client has an instant answer to this question, it is usually a traumatic life event that marked the end of one period in life and the beginning of another (i.e., Dad dying, the divorce, the bankruptcy, the fire, etc.).

Next, we come to questions in the present. These questions assume that you've already been through a history dialogue and that a level of understanding has been accomplished.

What does this money represent to you?

When a client brings an amount for you to invest on their behalf, prepare yourself for what you might hear. One adviser told Mitch the first time he asked this question, the man had laid down a check for $400,000 that he wanted to invest. His answer to this question was,

"This money represents four months in traction, and you'd better not lose a single cent." The adviser told Mitch he was glad he had asked.

Do you feel you're using your money to get the life you want, or is the pursuit of money keeping you from the life you want?
How much is your paycheck costing you?

We often think about what we are getting from our paychecks, but the "shadow" side of this question is more important for those who feel their working life is misguided or entirely on the wrong track.

Do you feel that your values are reflected within your investments?

This topic will be dealt with more extensively in chapter 15.

How will you know when you have enough?

We will be conducting a much deeper dive on this question and topic in the last chapter of this book. After all, it's only equitable that if we are questioning *if* they have enough (when they are shy of their goal), we should also be asking *when* and *how* they will know they *do* have enough.

Finally, we come to questions for the unfolding future. These questions are largely tied to life transitions ahead in a client's life. We will discuss a process for a thorough inquiry and dialogue on all life transitions in chapter 13.

Is there anything happening now or in the near future that you feel could have a major impact on your financial future?
If you already had the all the money you ever wanted, what would you do differently?

Ask this question to find out what really matters to the client:

In the 24-hour period between year 64, day 365, and year 65, day 1, what actually changes?

Ask this question when you want to bring a reality check regarding retirement into your discussion:

What observations have you made watching other people retire?

We will introduce a profile in chapter 14 that leads to a more granulated discussion on this topic.

How do I go back to old clients with these questions?

This is a question we often hear from advisers who, in the past, may have come up short in their discovery questions and are a bit embarrassed because they feel like they should know more about their clients' lives.

The simplest, most tactful answer to this question we can offer is, "You know, Mr. Client, when I saw you were coming in today it suddenly dawned on me that I don't know if I ever asked you, _____."

Then ask the question you wish you had asked before. No one is offended when you seek to learn more about them. In fact, they are usually flattered and eager to share their answer with you, no matter when you inquire. Clients are always happy to know that you are interested in them—and that's the key to relationships that grow. As we mentioned earlier in the chapter, instead of trying to demonstrate how interesting you may be, seek to demonstrate how interested you are.

Notice we started with the history before asking about goals. Have you ever gotten the deer-in-the-headlights look from prospects when you asked about their goals? Many don't know what their goals are because they are caught up in the present and haven't formalized a plan for the future.

Our view is that you haven't yet earned their trust to let you into their future. Start by going back first. Earn their respect by learning their formative story. It's important to ask the right questions—and it's equally as important to ask those questions in the right order.

Notes

1. Wildacres Leadership Initiative. https://www.fridayfellowship
.org/page/Dialogues.
2. Scott McDowell, "Five Common Reasons You Tune People Out," *Fast Company*. April 10, 2015. https://www.fastcompany.com/3044890/5-common-reasons-you-tune-people-out.

Chapter 10
Delivering Reality Checks

The truth does not change according to our ability to stomach it.
—Flannery O'Connor

Reality Check 1: Your Clients Need to Know Where Their Money Is Going

Mitch remembers having an interesting conversation with an astute financial planner named Bryan who was lamenting the shortcomings of goals-based approaches to financial planning. Here's what Bryan said to Mitch: "When we deal with clients on a goals-based approach without conducting an extensive cash flow analysis, we miss way too much of the real picture. I prefer to approach clients first and foremost on a cash flow basis before we ever bring goals into the conversation."

We think he's absolutely correct.

But, Houston, we have a problem.

For the past few years Mitch has been surveying all the advisers and planners in his speaking audiences (between 20,000 and 30,000 each year) and has asked them, "How many of you are conducting a lifetime cash flow analysis with your clients?" Can you guess the average response? How about less than 5%? To which we say, "If the boat is sinking, it just might have a leak."

When Mitch asked advisers why they didn't pursue this practice more, he heard the following:

- Clients really *don't want to know* what they're spending. They are living in ignorance—and for the time being, ignorance is bliss.
- When a cash flow analysis was provided, clients wouldn't provide accurate information— so essentially, the exercise was futile. Garbage in, garbage out.

Consequently, many advisers have given up on the effort. This is a mistake if you truly want to help your clients make progress. You can't measure progress without first benchmarking *where a client is right now*—and you can't build confidence upon a false premise.

Client Habits

It's not just a client's financial status that a detailed cash flow analysis exposes; it is that client's regimen and habits—the forces that either create wealth or impede its creation. As an adviser, you need to know as much as possible about a client's habits. In fact, what you learn may change your mind about whether or not you really want an individual for a client.

When you talk to a doctor, he or she does not cut the conversation short after finding out your current status. A good MD will inquire into your health regimen and health habits. They ask questions about how much you work out, eat, drink, smoke, and more. While many patients lie when answering these questions, doctors don't stop asking—they just try to get a sense for who is telling the truth. Here is a short list of the regimens and habits you'll want to be privy to:

- *Automated savings.* How much hands-free *saving* is going on? The more, the better. What aspects of their savings and investment program have been automated?
- *Monthly spending.* This is where you might meet the greatest resistance. Some practitioners ask for a general "guesstimate"

and then follow up with, "Would you like me to do some home-work and tell you how close you are to your guesstimate?"

- *Large purchases.* "How often do you make large purchases? Can you give me an example of your last two or three, and how you decided to make those purchases?"
- *Travel and entertainment.* "What would you guess you spend a year on travel and entertainment? Do you have a second home, timeshare, or regular vacation habit and budget?"
- *Giving habits.* "Are there any charities that you support on a yearly or monthly basis? What do you estimate your annual giv-ing to be? Do you have any charitable aspirations that you're aiming toward?"

Sometimes clients benefit most from the conversation they want to have the least. As one planner told us, "From my experience, if someone is a spender before they retire, that doesn't magically change *after* they retire." This scenario looms large with 70,000 boomers reaching 65 years old each week in the United States alone. These boomers are going to carry their regimens and habits with them across that age marker—but with a static income working against their goals, given their habits. Something will have to give, and the first place to look is at spending patterns and habits.

We've spent a considerable amount of time mulling over this dilemma of incognizance facing the advice profession and the well-being of clients. For those planners who would like a more subtle approach for illustrating the impact of spending before actu-ally conducting a detailed cash flow analysis, Mitch has devised a nonconfrontational method that requires nothing more than a tax return to produce an illustration, *Owe-Grow-Live-Give* (more on this later in the chapter).

You can broaden the cash flow conversation with clients by starting the conversation with them using the following dialogue: "Something we've learned in our many years of financial advice is that a client's habits are more important than a client's assets. Those habits either create or erode wealth. If you don't mind, I'd like to ask you a few questions about your regimens and money habits."

Whereas some advisers struggle to get the facts about their clients' expenditures, Paul has been successfully obtaining detailed expenditure questionnaires from clients for years. He uses a powerful presentation explaining what proper life-centered financial planning is really all about: helping clients to get and keep the life they want without the fear of running out of money or dying with too much. Paul helps them understand how money is designed to help them do what they want to do in the time they have left on this planet. Clients then realize that life-centered financial planning is not about creating a strict budget (even though some clients might desperately need that)—instead, it's about designing a life. Understanding your clients' current and desired future expenditure requirements is important to help them identify, achieve, and maintain their current and future desired lifestyle.

The bottom line is this: if your clients have formed good habits, they'll have you to affirm their disciplines. They might squirm a bit, but they'll be better off for knowing. Again, they can't make progress until you know the place they're starting from.

Reality Check 2: Your Clients Need to Be Responsible for Their Own Assumptions

Oftentimes, when advising clients, and showing those clients what their financial future looks like using comprehensive lifetime cash flow modeling software, Paul will hear something like, "Ah, but you're forgetting about my inheritance" or "You're forgetting about the sale of my business." Sound familiar?

In other words, clients mention a one-off future inflow that might have a positive effect on what their financial future looks like. The trouble is, if you then include their assumption into your planning, it could appear to fix their problem. This could end up being a big mistake.

How do you handle this? Simple. Challenge their assumption by asking them something like, "What are the chances of selling your business for $X?"" or "How much inheritance are you expecting, and when?"

Try and put some doubt in their mind about the reality of that happening. Question them. Challenge them. As a life-centered financial planner, it's your responsibility to do so. You might find that the client will quickly concede and agree to a lower, more prudent figure to be on the safe side. Explain to clients that it's your job to challenge them in order to help them become, and remain, financially independent.

Financial Independence versus Financial Dependence

To explain to clients what financial independence really means, you could say something like, "Mr. Client, it is important to understand what I mean by financially independent. You see, if we include in your planning the assumption (for example, $2 million from the sale of your business) then you are no longer planning to be financially independent at all. You are planning to become *financially dependent* on the sale of your business. And, quite simply, if it doesn't happen, then you'll be in big trouble!"

Just communicating this to clients can often make them reconsider whether it is wise to include the assumption in their planning. It might even encourage them to further reduce the assumption, just to be on the safe side. But they might still want to include an assumption, and that's perfectly fine, as long as they understand what that assumption means. In fact, many times, Paul has told clients that he's happy to include their assumption, but he asks them to sign a piece of paper confirming their understanding.

He would grab a blank piece of paper and write out the following:

Dear Paul:
Please include in my financial planning assumptions the FACT that I WILL sell my business for $2 million in today's terms (20___), NET of tax, on my 60th birthday. Signed <Client> <Date>

Here's what you could say after showing them this statement: "If you could just sign this, I will be glad to include this in your financial plan. Just so you understand, Mr. Client, I'm a professional financial planner, so I can't include my clients' assumptions in the plans I develop for them without those clients guaranteeing that those assumptions will become reality. I trust you understand."

This will normally get a client's respect—and they'll be even more reasonable in the amount they wish to include because it becomes their responsibility, not yours. This approach works with statements you hear such as: "I'll sell my business for X," or "I'll receive an inheritance for X," or "I'll sell my house for X." All these assumptions are fine, as long as: (a) you test them, and (b) the client signs off on them. If they don't sign off on the assumptions when you first discuss it, be sure to communicate it in a cover letter or prominent paragraph in any advice/suitability report or printed financial plan.

Remember, financial independence means your clients downsize their house because they want to, not because they have to, and that they are in a position that if they work, it's because they want to, not because they have to.

You may hear a client comment about age as well: "My situation looks worse because you are planning to age 100. I won't live to age 100. I'll be dead by age 85." Again, you could respond with a similar note to the one above:

Dear Paul:
Please include in my financial plan the FACT that I will be dead by 85. Signed <Client> <Date>.

Our guess is that when they are held responsible for their own assumptions, your client will suddenly "get it."

Using the right lifetime cash flow modeling software properly, you have power. You can stand up to reckless assumptions like "my business is my pension." Clients say this because they don't want traditional product-based advice. They don't want to be sold a pension or other product; and let's face it—who does? But they *do* want to secure their future and become financially independent. It's your job to make that happen, in part by being brutally honest when necessary. Clients will trust (and recommend) you more if you are.

Reality Check 3: Your Clients Need to Understand That What They Do with Their Income Impacts Their Life Outcome

You are not competing with anyone else. You are only competing with yourself to do the best with whatever you have received.
                                                              —*L. Tom Perry*

Though many clients may be subconsciously resisting a reality check of their situation, *they need to know* where they are at financially. For Mitch, this dilemma was one that needed to be solved in a simple manner. For those planners who would like a more subtle approach for illustrating the impact of spending before actually conducting a detailed cash flow analysis, this approach is designed to show clients what they're spending—without asking them to disclose what they're spending. As briefly described earlier in the chapter, *Owe-Grow-Live-Give* (OGLG) is a nonconfrontational method requiring nothing more than a tax return to produce an illustration.

There are only four actions we can take with our money. Taxes and debt are monies that we *owe*, and savings and investments are monies that we *grow*. Lifestyle spending is money used for *living*, and charitable donations are monies used for *giving*. The technique used here involves backing into a client's spending number by entering their *owe*, *grow*, and *give* numbers first, and voila—what's remaining is spending (*live*) because that's the only other way they could be using their money.

Owe-Grow-Live-Give helps clients recognize where they are regarding their personal allocation of income. This OGLG snapshot is available as an app but can just as easily be illustrated on a blank piece of paper or on the back of a napkin.

The conversation starts with the adviser inputting or writing down a client's annual income, then the amount they owe in mortgage debt and taxes (this is the *Owe* number). Next, input or write down their qualified savings number (this is the *Grow* number), and finally, input or write down their deductible contributions (this is the *Give* number). If you're doing this by hand, you'll have to do a little guesstimating to fill in these three categories appropriately in your hand-drawn circle. If you decide to use the app, the *Live* piece of the pie automatically populates (figure 10.1).

Clients are surprised when they see how much of the pie is lifestyle spending. This is a simple, noninvasive way to give clients a reality check.

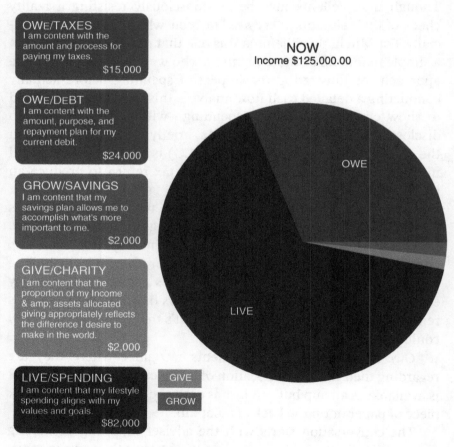

Figure 10.1   Owe-Grow-Live-Give: Now.

The *Owe-Grow-Live-Give* app is available as part of a subscription to Myflptools.com.
SOURCE: Mitch Anthony.

After showing clients their results, you can start the conversation by asking the following questions:

"Is there anything about this pie chart you'd like to change?"
"Are you surprised by anything?"
"What would you like to change?"

After this conversation, the next step is to explore where your clients would like to be. With the app, you simply input a goal in terms of years (in figure 10.2, we've used two years), and then adjust the income and the *Owe, Grow, Live,* and *Give* numbers to where your client would like them to be in that time frame. Now clients can view where are they now with where they want to be. Your conversation can now focus on the following questions:

"What steps will we need to take to get you there?"
"Here are some of my recommendations ... "

To truly make progress financially, clients must recognize the constant competition at work in their wallets between owing, growing, living, and giving. As an example, let's say one of your clients received an unexpected windfall of $10,000. OGLG now compete for those dollars.

Owe might say:

"Probably best to pay off the credit cards," or
"You could pay down your mortgage."

Grow will enter the debate and suggest:

"Finally, you can max out your retirement account this year—you've been saying you want to do that," or
"You know that $10,000 could be worth three times that in 10 years, if you could find a way to average 10%."

Live now enters the fray:

"You are *so* overdue for a nice weeklong trip to an exotic island," or

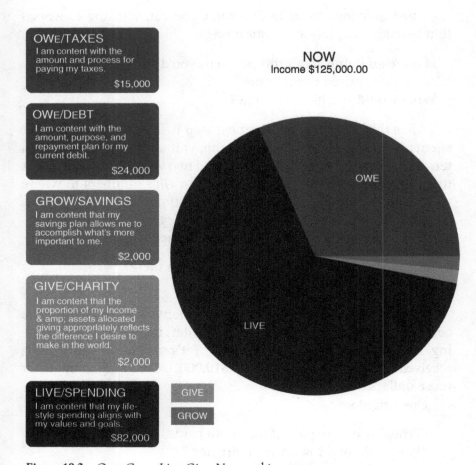

OWE/TAXES
I am content with the amount and process for paying my taxes.
$15,000

OWE/DEBT
I am content with the amount, purpose, and repayment plan for my current debit.
$24,000

GROW/SAVINGS
I am content that my savings plan allows me to accomplish what's more important to me.
$2,000

GIVE/CHARITY
I am content that the proportion of my Income & amp; assets allocated giving appropriately reflects the difference I desire to make in the world.
$2,000

LIVE/SPENDING
I am content that my life-style spending aligns with my values and goals.
$82,000

NOW
Income $125,000.00

OWE

LIVE

GIVE

GROW

Figure 10.2   Owe-Grow-Live-Give: Now and in two years.
SOURCE: Mitch Anthony.

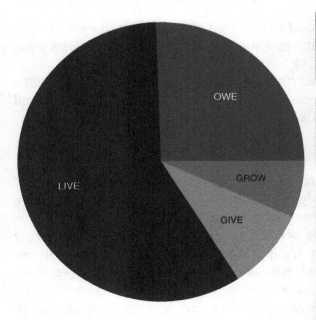

IN 2 YEARS
Income $150,000.00

OWE/TAXES
I am content with the amount and process for paying my taxes.
$20,000

OWE/DEBT
I am content with the amount, purpose, and repayment plan for my current debit.
$18,000

GROW/SAVINGS
I am content that my savings plan allows me to accomplish what's more important to me.
$10,000

GIVE/CHARITY
I am content that the proportion of my Income & amp; assets allocated giving appropriately reflects the difference I desire to make in the world.
$14,000

LIVE/SPENDING
I am content that my life-style spending aligns with my values and goals.
$88,000

"How long have you been waiting to buy that great couch for the living room? Sure, $10,000 is a lot for a couch, but this is like free money. Go for it!"

Give is trying to get into the discussion but is whispering so quietly that the others can hardly hear her talk:

"Wouldn't it be cool to take that money you never planned on having anyway and give it to the hurricane victims? How good would that feel?" or
"You want to really have some fun? How about taking $100 a week for 100 weeks, and then look for people who are in real need and just walk up and give it to them."

For all of us, the debate goes on every day with every dollar—even if we are not fully tuned in to the signal of this debate. In many ways what we do with our money is a reflection of our hearts. Obviously, we can't give all our money away or we wouldn't be able to support our families or meet our obligations or prepare for future needs. We can't spend everything on living today (though many try to). We can't save every penny without becoming stingy and without enjoying some of the pleasures and comforts that money provides to our daily lives. And, obviously we can't owe every penny we earn and not be miserable in manifold ways.

If we look more closely at the relationship between Owing and Growing, Owing and Living, Living and Giving, and Growing and Giving we will see the intangible payoffs of wise decision-making around allocation. The relationships between these uses of money are real, and we experience the competitive pressure they exert on a weekly and monthly basis.

From these four relationships we see the four outcomes that constitute what each client's "best life" looks like. These four relationships make up the Return on Life Dashboard—a method by which we can measure your client's progress toward achieving the best life financially:

1. The relationship between Owing and Growing has to do with *freedom*. If we owe the majority of our income, we are in bondage to those we owe. Our money is not really our own.
2. The relationship between Owing and Living has to do with *comfort*. We can have a really nice lifestyle, but if we are mortgaged to the hilt, we are under constant stress.
3. The relationship between Living and Giving has to do with *purpose*. If we are spending money and not deriving satisfaction from those expenditures, we could find more meaningful uses for those dollars.
4. The relationship between Growing and Giving has to do with *abundance*. There are many clients who already have more than they could ever spend but live in fear of not having enough should a crisis come down the road. They could be experiencing abundance by understanding what their charitable potential really is.

Allow us to frame it this way: if you could find a method for decision-making around money that delivered freedom, comfort, purpose, and abundance into your life, would that financial framework be worth considering? Keep in mind that the antitheses of these results are bondage, stress, aimlessness, and lack—which none of us aim for.

We experience cognitive, emotional, and even spiritual breakthrough when we come to realize that what we do with our money impacts our heart and the very quality of our existence. Who doesn't want a life replete with freedom, comfort, purpose, and abundance? Wise financial decisions can trigger and perpetuate all four of these features into our daily lives ... but it all starts with an examination of where our money is going.

The adviser who can be trusted over all others is the adviser who is not afraid to administer the appropriate, and timely, reality check. The lesson is simple: life outcomes hinge very tightly on how we manage our incomes.

Part III

The Dialogues of the Future

Chapter 11
What's Your Fiscalosophy?

The past is prologue.

—*William Shakespeare*

How did your clients come by their attitudes, beliefs, behaviors, and habits around money? Is it by chance or by happenstance? We would like to put forth the idea that there are both blueprints and fingerprints regarding each client's attitude and habit-forming around money. By blueprints we mean those formative experiences of growing up, and by fingerprints we mean the personal experiences and observations gathered in an individual's journey with money.

To arrive at this knowledge of your client requires a unique skill set—that of a biographer. In fact, your competence in all matters of discovery comes down to developing this biographical competency with your clients and their stories. Where the majority of the profession is trying to put together a story of numbers, the wise adviser is busy gathering a number of stories. Why? Because the stories are the very context for the numbers; they give the numbers meaning.

The chief characteristic required to exercise your inner biographer is curiosity, plain and simple. Do you believe that people are basically the same, or do you believe, even though there may be similarities, they are absolutely unique creatures with idiosyncratic stories to tell? If you believe the latter, then it is incumbent upon you, the story-gatherer, to excavate the stories that spell out that personal uniqueness. But before we go further with what the curious inquirer ought to ask, we must address the *organic order of the story*, that is, where should one inquire first, second, and so on.

Organically Speaking

If we were tasked with writing your biography, we would begin our inquiry with your *past story*: "Where did you grow up?" "Tell us about your family." "What did your parents do?" "What was money like growing up?" "Where did you go to school, and what were your interests?" "What was your first job?" "What did you study to become, and how did you get to where you are today?" "Where did you meet your mate?"

Then (very naturally) we arrive at the present; this is where all of yesterday's stories bring us to. Here we ask: "How long have you lived here, and what brought you?" "Tell me about your current work." "What kind of involvement do you have in the community?" "Do you like it here?"

Lastly, in the biographical context, we would ask about your future: "What do you want to be when you grow up?" "How long do you envision doing what you're doing now?" "Is retirement a goal for you?" "What happens when the kids are all grown up?" "How do you hope to leave a mark in this world?"

One thing is for sure: if you ask this set of questions to the next 100 people you meet, no two answers will be the same. Each of us has our own journey. It behooves the life-centered financial planner to understand that journey. In this chapter we will share not only some questions to help you understand your client's story, but we will also introduce a discovery tool to help you organize your clients' perspectives, and know where to start to help them and their story turn out the way they wish. In fact, this chapter and the two that follow are all a part of the story-gathering process. This chapter is concerned with the past story, the next will deal with the present story, and the chapter after that will focus on the future and unfolding story.

We have noted that far too many advisers are not practicing what we would call the *organic order of discovery*: start with history, move naturally into the present, and after that, discuss the possibilities for the future. Many in this profession start by talking about goals and then move back into the present, largely ignoring the past.

On another note about discovery techniques, we question the wisdom of going too deep too early when getting to know clients. We're all for going deeper into meaningful dialogues with clients, but opening with a "what is the meaning of life" question brings an awkwardness to both the questioner and the respondent. We know there will be some who disagree with us on this point, but we posit this from the standpoint of talking to many advisers who attempted such techniques, only to see them backfire.

Past→Path Forward→Pathos

Regarding the past story, allow us to remind you of what you want to discover more than anything: the inspiration or the pathos that has directed their life to this point.

One question that cuts to the quick of this type of discovery is, "Have you had any experiences that you would call a *defining experience?*" This is where you hear about Dad dying, the fire, the divorce, the bankruptcy—traumatic life experiences that deeply impacted their blueprint in life. When you ask specifically about money, the following questions have proven to be excellent igniters for dialogue:

"What was money like growing up?"
"When you think back to when you were young, what is the first recollection that comes to you about money?"
"What would you describe as your best and worst experiences with money so far?"
"Have you had any experiences with other financial professionals, good or bad, that would be worth your time to tell me about?"

These questions lead to rich dialogues regarding the formative experiences and sometimes inhibiting and confusing experiences that stay with the fiscal psyche and continue to show up in decision after decision. You don't have to be a therapist to ask these questions. If the client exhibits a pronounced fiscal phobia or psychosis, it would be helpful to have a counselor to refer them to. Your interest in their story is not for therapeutic purposes but for biographical purposes—to understand what makes your clients tick.

Understanding Their Drivers

- Theodore believes that the only money that is really yours is the money you spend.
- Debra believes that every person, no matter how good, is susceptible to a personal demon of greed.
- Richard believes that you can never be sure of having enough.

Let's assume for a moment that these three people are your clients and that your goal is to establish and maintain a full-scale and long-term advisory relationship with all of them. Chances are you already have clients like these, whether or not you have heard these sentiments. And you might have witnessed behaviors that reveal their underlying beliefs:

- Theodore spends large sums of cash to go on trips and have experiences.
- Debra shows a hesitance and reluctance to act on your advice.
- Richard is financially anxious and exhibits a high level of scrutiny that seems inappropriate given his net worth.

Why do Theodore, Debra, and Richard believe and feel the way they do in critical areas of financial management? We learn the following things from them in an interview:

- Theodore believes that the only money that is really yours is that which you spend, because his father, a man who worked extremely hard seven days a week, never took time to really enjoy what he earned.

- Debra believes that even the best people must fight with the demons of greed. When her first husband died, he had forgotten to switch the assignment of the life insurance benefit from his parents to his new bride, and her in-laws kept the money.
- Richard believes that you can never be sure you have enough, even though he is a multimillionaire. He grew up in a large family with 11 children that his father struggled to support, working 14 hours a day. The family was evicted from three different homes.

Fiscalosophy: a. what one believes about money; b. a set of principles or guidelines for managing one's financial affairs.

To begin this dialogue, we must start by understanding a few truisms:

- Belief systems drive behaviors.
- Belief systems are shaped by experiences.
- Beliefs are philosophies constructed with what we conclude are fundamental principles for success.
- We feel greater kinship with those who share our beliefs.

You are dealing with and managing the fruit of your client's fiscal philosophy every day. But do you know how your client began thinking in a way that drives his specific behavior?

Our recommendation is that if you apply yourself to the second and third items (understanding the experiences that shaped your client's beliefs and facilitating a discussion about the fundamental principles for financial success), you will achieve greater agility and expediency in terms of building agreement and long-term kinship with clients who are aligned with you.

Clients can feel palpable stress if they don't have a sense of agreement or alignment with their advisers. If they have a suspicion that the person they have entrusted their assets to is not on the same page, they experience a churning in the gut. They wonder what they should do and where they should go. That discomfort will ease only when they have a big-picture philosophical discussion with

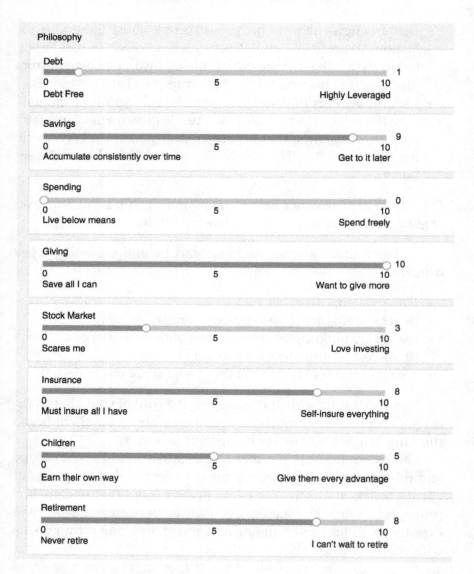

Figure 11.1 Sample Fiscalosophy Profile.
SOURCE: Mitch Anthony.

Comfort Level

Level of Debt

0 — Very Comfortable | 5 | 10 — Very Uncomfortable | 10

Level of Savings

0 — Very Comfortable | 5 | 10 — Very Uncomfortable | 10

Level of Spending

0 — Very Comfortable | 5 | 10 — Very Uncomfortable | 1

Level of Giving

0 — Very Comfortable | 5 | 10 — Very Uncomfortable | 1

Stock Market Exposure

0 — Very Comfortable | 5 | 10 — Very Uncomfortable | 2

Coverage of Insurance Risks

0 — Very Comfortable | 5 | 10 — Very Uncomfortable | 6

Level of Children Support

0 — Very Comfortable | 5 | 10 — Very Uncomfortable | 3

Idea of Retirement

0 — Very Comfortable | 5 | 10 — Very Uncomfortable | 2

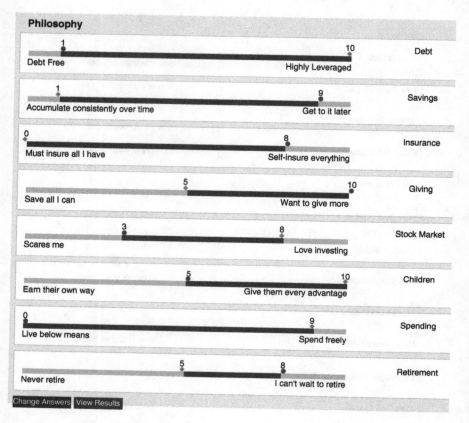

Figure 11.2 Example variance report.
SOURCE: Mitch Anthony.

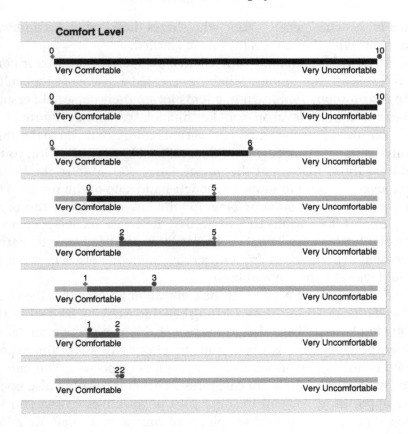

an adviser who "gets it"—one who shares their principles and who connects with the lessons they have learned.

To better understand your clients' perspectives and their comfort levels around money, Mitch has created a discovery tool called the *Fiscalosophy Profile*. In it, clients locate their personal perspectives and comfort level on eight key financial categories (figure 11.1).

The areas that show up in the various colors alert you to the areas your client or prospect is most uncomfortable with, allowing you to address those matters at the outset. Once you address their comfort level, it's time to move to the left-hand side of the report. This is the time to put on your biographer's hat so that you can begin to pinpoint the reasons they arrived at their various perspectives in the eight categories. People arrive at their perspectives either from personal experience or from observing someone else's experience. You'll want to know about both.

For example, if we look at the Debt slider and see that the client placed it near 0 (indicating a strong belief in carrying no debt at all), you simply ask, "How did you arrive at this perspective on debt?" Now the story door is open, and the client will share the experience(s) and observations that led to this perspective. You can do this with each of the eight categories. This conversation also opens the opportunity for you to share *your* perspectives (when you see true alignment) and to share pieces of *your story* as well. Relationship development is the result of the exchange of story. Keep that in mind as motivation for digging deeper and disclosing elements of your story as well.

The final aspect of the Fiscalosophy Profile process is the *variance report*—a tool designed for couples to fill out the profile individually. The report shows the adviser how close together—or far apart—the couple is on perspectives and comfort levels. A partial sample of the variance can be seen in figure 11.2, where one partner's views are represented by a circle and the other represented by a diamond.

We want to remind you that this tool is designed primarily for personal awareness purposes, meaning clients are going to learn something interesting about themselves, and in an articulation they have never seen before. This will give the couple some interesting fodder to go home and discuss. They will need to discuss how to make the necessary negotiations to move forward, if there is too wide a separation in their perspectives. If such variances exist, they were already aware of it, no doubt—this just brings the tacit reality to the surface.

The secondary purpose of the profile is for you: an awareness of who you are dealing with and how the couple arrived at the place they are with their money. Don't worry, you don't have to play marriage counselor if they are miles apart on the variance report, but you may well save a marriage if you can bring recommendations that help them both feel more comfortable with their financial situation. We all know the role money plays in relationships floundering or flourishing, as it is consistently a leading driver to the divorce courts.

Do you understand your clients' philosophies on investments and money matters? Do you understand the experiences that shaped (and continue to shape) their views? If not, you may find out when it's too late, and they've left for another adviser. Do your clients understand your fiscal philosophy and the inviolable principles that you believe in? Most important, do you and your clients share the same fiscalosophy? Your clients' beliefs and principles regarding money will be reflected in their behavior, and it can be an ideal advisory relationship if you are both on the same page (if possible)—and if you are not on the same page, then this fact is clearly demonstrated.

Chapter 12

What Is Your Return on Life?

Many folks think they aren't good at earning money, when what they don't know is how to use it.

—*Frank A. Clark*

If you want to change the dynamics of the financial relationship to a value that is most meaningful, start by changing the central question being answered in that relationship. The core question driving the advice and planning world has been, "Do you or will you have enough money?" On Paul's side of the pond the question is more likely, "Are you making the most of your money?" Little wonder then that advisers spend so much time validating allocations, investments, and returns, thereby creating a never-ending cul-de-sac dynamic where they must constantly justify how they are doing on a relative basis—resulting in a game no one can win.

As we've discussed throughout this book, in life-centered financial planning the central objective is getting a greater Return on Life (ROL), not just getting a greater return on investment (ROI). The central question is *not*, "Do you have enough money?" or "Are you making the most of your money?" Instead, the central question is, "Are you getting the best life possible with the money you have?" This question places the emphasis where it belongs: *on behaviors that produce results*. The ROL paradigm places the planner in a

seat of true advice when weighing in with wisdom on the financial
behaviors and principles that need to be applied to better a client's
situation.

Mitch has spent the last few years investigating exactly what
"getting the best life possible" looks like. What are the chief components of a quality life tied directly to financial decision-making?
His research revealed there are 10 aspects of life tied to financial dis-
cretion and prudence, all of which constitute the three categories of
what most would agree is a "quality life":

1. A sense of well-being
2. The sense that you're making progress
3. The sense that you have freedom to live life the way you want

The next challenge was to identity the aspects of life—impacted
by financial behavior—that contribute to well-being, a sense of
progress, and freedom to live the life you want.

In Exhibit 12.1, you will see the 10 aspects of life that constitute
the *Return on Life Index* (ROL Index).

The final challenge, after identifying the 10 aspects contributing to a greater Return on Life, was to figure out a way
for clients and prospective clients to measure their situational
progress against these 10 aspects. We concluded that people need
to measure where they are presently against the ideals they are
striving for in the context of Return on Life. This is how the ROL
Index was born.

The ROL Index will help clients answer the question, "Am I
getting the best life possible with the money I have?"—the very
definition of Return on Life. For each of the 10 contributing aspects,
we designed both a financial and a lifestyle question that impacts
success in each aspect of life. Clients are given the opportunity
to assign a numeric value to their perception of progress in each
of these areas. Our hope in advancing the Return on Life (or
life-centered planning) paradigm is to remove focus on comparative market measures and place attention and focus on personal
progress, which is better for both client and planner.

In the following description of ROL components, we list
the 10 aspects impacting well-being, progress, and freedom. For
each aspect, you will see the questions addressing both financial
and lifestyle contributors to success. Each aspect is articulated

in simple, clear language and followed by two key contributing factors. Finally, we offer sample questions (both financial and lifestyle-oriented) for clients to ponder if they are truly seeking to improve each of these aspects of their lives.

In the digital form of the index, the client can move the slider between 0 and 10 and will have a maximum value of 100 for each category (20 is multiplied by 5 in the calculation to get to the 100 value). This way, for each aspect of life, clients can see how close they are to optimizing their situation and also see how they are doing in the three main categories of life: well-being, progress, and freedom.

Figure 12.1 shows the questions clients answer for 3 of the 10 categories surveyed in the Return on Life Index. The first question is a lifestyle question and the second is a financial question. The two answers combine for the score they'll see in their final result (figure 12.2).

The results graphic the client sees will demonstrate the specific aspects of life impacting their well-being, sense of progress, and sense of freedom.

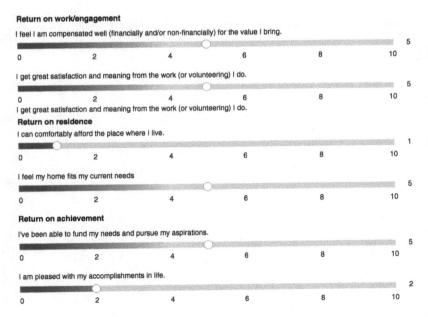

Figure 12.1   Sample ROL index questions.
SOURCE: Mitch Anthony

Completed on 05/18/2018 10:40 AM

43
ROL Index

36
Well-Being

Needs Attention
Your ROL Index indicates that there are areas where you could improve your satisfaction with some changes in how you manage your resources.

Your top two areas of highest ROL are **Autonomy, Work** and your lowest two ROL rankings were in **Residence, Leisure.**

Change Answers

Leisure **30**

Health **50**

Relationships **30**

Figure 12.2   Sample ROL index results.
SOURCE: Mitch Anthony

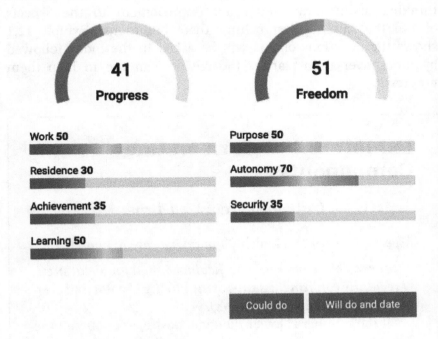

In discussing the results with clients, we have developed questions and conversation starters to prompt them to start thinking about how they bring improvement to the aspects of life that are lagging behind their intentions. Exhibit 12.1 shows the questions clients will be asked in the index followed by the conversation starters the adviser can use to help them progress.

Exhibit 12.1: Return on Life Components

Category One: *Well-Being*

Aspect 1: Return on Health ("I'm taking care of myself.")

I've been able to maintain my health without financial stress. I regularly confirm the status of my physical health and overall well-being with my doctor(s).

If the number is lower than you desire, ask yourself the following:

- "Do I have adequate health insurance?"
- "Am I proactively improving my health? Eating right? Regular exercise? Health club membership?"
- "Do I have a primary care physician?"
- "Do I get regular exams?"

Aspect 2: Return on Relationships ("I have a healthy relationship with my family and friends.")

My relationships have not been adversely affected by money matters.
I can afford to take care of the people I want to help.

If the number is lower than you desire, ask yourself the following:

- "Have I taken steps to educate children/grandchildren on wise money management?"
- "Have I made loans to family or friends that have introduced tension?"
- "Are my parents or any other family members in need of financial assistance?"
- "Do I (we) have transparency in household spending?"

Aspect 3: Return on Residence ("I'm in the place I want to be.")

I feel my home is the right place for me.
I can comfortably afford the place(s) where I live.
    If the number is lower than you desire, ask yourself the following:

- "Am I comfortable to stay in this home for the long-term future?"
- "Are there living options that might be more practical or enjoyable at this stage?"
- "Are the costs of residence easily managed?"
- "Are we interested in a second home or vacation rental for winter or summer months?"

Aspect 4: Return on Security ("I'm comfortable with my financial situation.")

I feel secure about my current financial situation.
I feel confident about my financial future.
    If the number is lower than you desire, ask yourself the following:

(continued)

(continued)

- "Do I (we) feel adequately insured with regard to health, home, and household possessions?"
- "Would my loved ones be able to maintain their lifestyle if I passed away?"
- "Am I involved in any investments I have reservations about?"
- "When is the last time I had my total wealth allocation reviewed?"

Category Two: *Progress*

Aspect 5: *Return on Learning ("I'm happy with my educational investments.")*

I feel I am effectively using my finances toward education.
I am involved in lifelong learning through reading, training, and association with others.

If the number is lower than you desire, ask yourself the following:

- "Have I conducted an analysis on the ROI of colleges for my child(ren)?" (if applicable)
- "Am I (we/family members) under strain regarding student loans?"
- "What investments would I like to make regarding my own growth and progress?"
- "Are there any learning experiences that I've been putting off?"

Aspect 6: *Return on Achievement ("I am getting things done.")*

I've been able to fund my needs and pursue my aspirations.

I am pleased with my accomplishments in life.

If the number is lower than you desire, ask yourself the following:

- "Are there things I would attempt if I had the funding?"
- "Do I feel I am at the place I want to be in life at this time?"
- "Are there obstacles holding me back from attempting something new?"
- "Can I see myself doing what I do for a long time to come?"

Aspect 7: Return on Leisure ("I am enjoying life.")

I've been able to fund my hobbies and interests.
I am taking the time to visit the places I like to see, do the things I like to do, and spend time with the people important to me.

If the number is lower than you desire, ask yourself the following:

- "Am I able to comfortably afford the memberships I have?"
- "Are there trips I want to make in the near future rather than later?"
- "Are there people far away that I want to visit soon?"
- "Are there new hobbies or interests that I've been putting off?"

Category Three: *Fulfillment*

Aspect 8: Return on Autonomy ("I'm doing what I want to do.")

I am utilizing my money in ways to help me free my time.

(continued)

(*continued*)

I feel freedom in my work, relationships, and how I live my life.

If the number is lower than you desire, ask yourself the following:

- "Have I made purchases that have caused stress in my life?"
- "Are there investments I'm in that make me uncomfortable?"
- "Am I feeling the freedom to do what I want in life?"
- "Do I have the time to attend to things that mean the most to me?"

Aspect 9: Return on Work/Engagement ("I feel good about the contributions I make.")

I feel I am compensated well (financially and/or nonfinancially) for the value I bring.
I get great satisfaction from the work I do.

If the number is lower than you desire, ask yourself the following:

- "Am I being compensated for what I feel I'm worth?"
- "Do I feel appreciated for what I bring with my efforts?"
- "Am I consistently energized by the work that I do?"
- "Do I get positive reinforcement for my efforts?"

Aspect 10: Return on Purpose ("I'm living with meaning.")

I am living my life "on purpose."
I feel I am able to live and give generously with my time, talents, and/or finances.

If the number is lower than you desire, ask yourself the following:

- "Do I desire to give more of my time and substance?"
- "Am I perfectly comfortable with the causes I do support?"
- "Are there charitable aspirations that I have not yet pursued?"
- "Are there causes I'd like to gain greater exposure to?"

Resetting the Focus

A planner who is using the ROL Index with all his prospects and clients recently told us that he was discussing the results with a couple he'd been working with for many years and who had been married for over 30 years. They turned to him after they'd discussed their results and said, "That is the best conversation we may have ever had in the 30 plus years we've been married." We take that as encouragement that clients actually desire a deeper, more meaningful dialogue around their finances. Talking about investments can never bring that kind of profound feeling to a relationship.

Mitch remembers taking a financial planner through the index and noticing that his autonomy number was very low (15). He asked the planner why that number was so low while all the others were relatively high. The planner responded, "That's because I love what I do, but I hate the place I work and don't like the people I work with."

"You can do something about that, can't you?' Mitch asked.

If this sort of dilemma is playing out for advisers, you can be sure it is playing itself out with clients as well. Having made it and having it made are two different matters. We must utilize our money in ways that enhance our lives; otherwise, we have failed in that particular respect.

The opportunity we're offering in the life-centered financial planning and ROL approach to the world of financial planning is

142   THE DIALOGUES OF THE FUTURE

to change the central question guiding the planning conversation. That central question has been about having enough money, getting a better return on investments, and making the most profit from your money. We must reiterate that the central question needs to be, *"Are you getting the best life possible with the money you have?"* This question places the emphasis where it belongs: on behaviors that produce results. The posturing of this question places the planner in a position of "wisdom merchant"—one who can weigh in on what financial behaviors and principles need to be applied to better a client's situation.

Change the central question you are attempting to answer, and the perception of your value will change with it. The ROL Index is an attempt at answering the questions that matter most to clients. In the next chapter we'll demonstrate how to personalize the planning process so that it is literally a *life portrait* of the client's situation. By taking this biographical path with clients, your relationship to clients will take on a whole new layer of meaning.

Chapter 13
Money in Motion

I figured something out. The future is unpredictable.
—John Green

Focus on your clients' goals.
Find out where they want to be.
Help them achieve their dreams.

Such phrases have become half mantra/half cliché in the modern advisory world. If you're smart, you'll build your client conversations around something other than pie in the sky and get focused on what matters in the undeniable here and now.

Have you ever asked a client what his or her goals are, only to be met with that deer-in-the-headlights response? Most people are so caught up in the present that they haven't yet framed a portrait for the future. Goals are an important conversation, but they need to be addressed at the right time and in the proper context.

The fragile, the fickle and frivolous, whimsical musings, and capricious contexts are no place to build the foundation for a life-centered advisory relationship. There is a place for a "goals" conversation—we just don't believe it is in the initial, formative stage of the relationship. And there is also some industry baggage around the "What are your goals and dreams?" conversation: it has been routinely used as a launching pad for cheap salesmanship by people masquerading as advisers. A better place than goals to commence a conversation that will last is in the realm of life transitions—the changes, passages, and concerns taking place in the here and now—the real-life episodes clients are encountering on the road of life.

The fundamental difference between goals and transitions is this:

- Goals are what we want to happen.
- Transitions are what is happening anyway.

It's a matter of focusing on the things that *are* happening, not just the things that we *want* to happen. It has been said, "If you want to make God laugh, show Him your five-year plan." Life is what happens while we are making our plans. Do you want to anchor your advisory relationships on the events that will happen or on those that might happen? Better think about it because your answer today will determine whether you exist on a foundation of rock or sand 10 years from now.

Connect on the basis of the inevitable, not just on wishful thinking. The truth is, many of your clients' goals are not going to come to pass. Life is going to get in the way. Parents are going to age, need assistance, and restrict your clients logistically and financially. There are going to be health challenges. Children are going to grow up, move on, move back, and continue to bring challenges into your clients' lives. Companies are going to "change directions," pensions are going to get halved or disappear altogether, and entire professions are going to become automated. The best-laid investment plans and the markets are not obliged to go along with our goals and hopes. The only thing that is certain in life is that life will certainly change. And while life is changing direction, it is not necessarily taking its cues from our turn signal or intentions.

As advisers, we are much better off asking clients what their concerns are, what passages of life they are going through, and what changes they see coming than we are spouting the trite and overused, "Tell me about your goals."

What Was I Thinking?

One day Mitch was rummaging through old files and came across a goals sheet that he had been cajoled into filling out in a workshop.

All the participants had been given dire directives at the time about the necessity of: (1) writing down your goals, and (2) keeping those goals in front of you. Mitch doesn't remember the exact statistics the instructor gave, but the odds were somewhere between the penthouse and the outhouse if he failed to subscribe to these commandments. So, Mitch wrote down his goals and promptly misplaced them—he didn't come across them until five years later. And after reading the list, he had to thank goodness and fate that he had lost those goals in such prompt fashion. Why? In retrospect Mitch's goals fell into two neat categories:

1. *Already happened* (even without ever having looked at them again)
2. *"What was I smoking at the time?"* (How could Mitch have ever convinced himself that he actually wanted *that* to happen?)

Mitch began to reflect on what a goal really was. If a goal was truly a goal, wouldn't it take root organically and grow? And if it wasn't a goal—and instead a whim or capricious desire—wouldn't the winds of personal awareness blow it away to some other garden? Many of our so-called goals change as often as the fashion world. I think of the whimsicality of goals every time I hear the adage, "the two best days in a boat owner's life: the day you buy your boat and the day you sell it."

Come Back from the Future: Life Transitions

For advisers intent on building serious lifetime relationships, conversations about goals and dreams are not the place to start—they are too fuzzy, too elusive, too susceptible to impulse and fad to suffice as the foundational dialogue in that relationship. Instead, build that foundation with clients on the here and now: the coming-soon-to-a-life-near-you realities, concerns, and transitions of everyday life.

For the past two decades the Financial Life Planning Institute (FLPI), founded by Mitch, has been researching both life transitions and life goals, as well as their impact on financial well-being. The bottom line, the FLPI has discovered, is that advisers are much better off getting in touch and staying in touch with their clients' transitions first—as those are the issues that have the greatest impact on their financial status and well-being at that moment.

The FLPI research has uncovered 60 life transitions that we can expect to take place between the birth and death. As individuals, we do not pass through all of these transitions because of our unique family and career circumstances, but we will pass through a multitude of transitions in our lifetime. These transitions fall into six categories:

1. Personal/family
2. Health
3. Career/work
4. Retirement-related
5. Financial/investment
6. Community/legacy transitions

The FLPI conducted comprehensive research on each life transition that has provided advisers access to information regarding the general considerations, discovery questions, financial implications, and educational resources around each of the 60 life transitions.

Once your clients indicate their chief concerns, you are able to engage them in a meaningful conversation about what they need to think about to navigate successfully through specific life transitions. This conversation is centered on the "here and now" and the "coming soon" aspects of their life. Built within this conversation system is the implied urgency to act because quality of life is on the line for themselves and their loved ones.

After surveying more than 3,000 advisory clients on their "top 10" life concerns, we found it interesting that many of these concerns are rarely mentioned in the typical adviser/client conversation or in the typical financial industry literature. A classic example of this is *concern about an aging parent*—a top concern but one scarcely surveyed by the average adviser.

To look at literature from most firms, one would assume there are only three transitions or concerns in life (college, retirement, and death) rather than 65. Could it be the industry at large lacks the education to engage in meaningful conversations about the other aspects of life—or lacks the imagination to see how their products and services could be utilized to meet the needs of these transitions? We suspect it is both.

A director of training for a prominent firm in the financial services industry made a pithy observation on the dearth of real-life advice regarding a recent life transition he and his wife recently experienced: their daughter's marriage. This director told Mitch, "We just experienced the biggest financial distribution we will probably ever experience, and we were in no way, shape, or form prepared for the impact. Not only did we see our investable assets take a major hit, but our plans for the future are profoundly impacted as well. This is a conversation we wish we would have had ahead of time."

The Here and Now, and Near Horizon

The most prudent place to focus your primary attention is what is happening in the here and now, and what is on the near horizon; or, in other words, on real life as it unfolds before your client's eyes. There is plenty of opportunity right in front of you. With this focus, there will continue to be opportunity because life is dynamic—every time life shifts, there may be a need to respond financially to that shift.

Life transitions impact both the well-being of your client and the well-being of your practice:

- There is an umbilical relationship between *life being in transition* and *money being in motion*.
- *It is better to prepare than to repair.* Much self-sabotaging financial behavior could be avoided by proactively addressing life transitions.
- A *personalized financial plan* must address the transitions unique to the client being planned for.

As mentioned above, if one were to listen in on most advice discussions, one would quickly conclude there are only a handful of life transitions that need to be planned for and around. To some degree, this modality of thinking can be traced back to the products that financial services manufacturers have offered: insurance products, savings vehicles, and finance products. As a consequence, the transitions most commonly addressed have been children going to college, retirement, purchasing homes, and death. But life passages are much broader and more voluminous than this short list; if we ignore the other passages, we do so to our own undoing.

Transitioning to Transitions

In life-centered financial planning, specific life transitions that your client is facing at the moment and anticipating in the future make up the spinal column of the planning dialogue. This aspect makes your process highly personalized and uniquely vital to a *client's* reality.

It is not the planner's job to determine what priority each transition should occupy—that is the responsibility of the client. But the planner is required to:

- Be aware of key life transitions
- Offer proactive financial guidance
- Monitor changes that would impact the client's unique situation

There are six categories of transitions that need to be queried, and a total of 60 transitions in these six life categories. A discussion of all 60 transitions goes well beyond the scope of this book. However, if you are interested in a method for tracking clients' transitions, you may want to look at the following illustrations from the Financial $Lifeline (available at ROLAdvisor.com). If not interested, just skip ahead to the section on The Ongoing Conversation.

Figure 13.1 is a sample of the *Financial $Lifeline*. In this sample, Michael and his wife Jackie charted out various transitions they are approaching in the next decade or so. The various icons

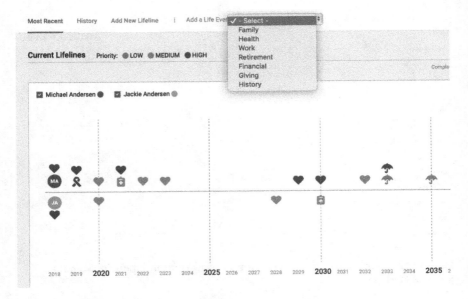

Figure 13.1   Sample Financial $Lifeline.
SOURCE: Mitch Anthony.

represent the different categories of transition (i.e., health-related, family-related, work-related).

First, the clients' ages and estimates of how long they might live are entered. After choosing the Personal/Family icon, a list of personal and family transitions unique to Michael and Jackie is revealed (see figure 13.2). Their adviser then asks them to prioritize between low, medium, and high, and then drags the various transitions to the appropriate location on their Financial $Lifeline (which is also confirmed verbally by the adviser).

When the life transition identification process is completed, the clients' Financial $Lifeline will be populated by the most important (and deeply emotive) aspects of their life.

The Financial $Lifeline summary in figure 13.3 becomes your ROL agenda going forward. No more wondering what you're going to discuss with a client at this review because the client's personal lifeline dictates the dialogue. This is client-centric, personalized

To add a Life Event, drag and drop it onto a year on the Lifeline below

	Low	Medium	High
Getting married			
Divorce / separation			
Entering single parenthood			
Loss of spouse			
Expecting a child			
Adopting a child			
Hiring childcare			
Child with special needs			
Child getting married			
Empty nest			
Special family event			
Assistance to a family member			
Relocating			
Child going to college			

Figure 13.2   Sample of personal and family transitions in Financial $Lifeline.
SOURCE: Mitch Anthony.

☑ Mitch anthony ●   ☑ Deb Anthony ◉

2020	MA		**Work** (Gain / lose a business partner)
2021	MA		**Work** (Expand business)
2023	DA		**Health** (Concern about an aging parent)
2024	DA	♥	**Family** (Empty nest)
2024	MA	♥	**Family** (Empty nest)
2024	MA		**Retirement** (Downshift worklife)
2025	DA	$	**Financial** (Purchasing a home)
2026	DA	♥	**Family** (Assistance to a family member)
2026	DA	♥	**Family** (Empty nest)
2026	MA		**Retirement** (Start receiving Social Security income)
2027	DA		**Work** (Selling / closing a business)
2028	MA		**Retirement** (Start receiving retirement plan distributions)
2030	DA		**Retirement** (Changing residence)

Figure 13.3   Sample Financial $Lifeline summary.
SOURCE: Mitch Anthony.

planning at its absolute best. One observation made by a planner using a transition focus has been that once you place the searchlight on your clients' transitions, they intuitively understand the need to keep you in the loop of any upcoming changes in their situation. You are now more than a financial adviser—you are a *financial life confidant.*

Now your work as a life-centered financial planner kicks in. Step one is getting the story. Click on the transition being discussed, and a discovery path appears. The devil is in the details, and no details will be glossed over as you learn the intricacies and nuances of their particular passage. With the Financial $Lifeline you are supplied both with educational content for the client (figure 13.4) and a discovery path for your discussion (figure 13.5)

2. Doctors
If you are concerned with the health of an aging parent, the first thing you should do is to talk with a medical professional. Doctors and nurses can diagnose problems in the early stages and offer treatments if needed. They can also sit down with you and explain your parent's specific needs.

3. Familiarizing yourself with your parents' needs
If your parent has a specific problem such as Alzheimer's, heart disease, or other problems that affect the elderly, be sure to research the condition. There are a variety of resources available on the internet and in the bookstore. Understanding your parent's needs will help alleviate your anxiety and guide you in providing care.

4. Organizations that can help
There are a number of organizations created for helping the elderly and their families. These include the American Association for Retired Persons (AARP), the National Council on the Aging, and the National Senior Citizens Law Center. Another helpful site is Eldercare, a public service of the U.S. Administration on Aging. Their link is: http://eldercare.gov/Eldercare.NET/Public/Index.aspx

Many communities have Senior Centers where you can go to familiarize yourself with the needs of senior citizens and the resources available in your community. All of these organizations can provide you with helpful hints on caring for an elderly parent in both a loving and economical way.

5. Communicating with your parent
Talk to your parent about your concern. Ask if there is anything you can do to help them overcome the challenges of aging. Your parent may just be looking for someone to voice concerns to or may need someone's advice. Take into consideration your parent's needs and desires. Encouraging communication is an important step in laying groundwork for future aid.

6. Communicating with others
If you have become concerned about a parent's wellbeing, you are probably not alone. Talk to other family members, friends, and neighbors. They might be able to alleviate your concerns or provide helpful insights. Remember, the larger your resource network, the better care you can provide.

7. Support for you
Realizing that your parent may be going through a difficult time can be an emotionally stressful situation for you to handle. Talk to other members of your family and other people you know who have gone through the same thing. Securing emotional support for yourself will help you deal with the stress and concerns you might have. As always, seek professional help or the assistance of support groups if needed.

8. Personnel needs
Many times, elderly parents need extra help, such as housecleaning or grocery shopping. If you are not able to provide the assistance yourself, think about hiring someone who can. Think about local cleaning agencies or programs such as Meals-on-Wheels offered in your community. As your parent gets older or if he/she is suffering from an illness, you may consider hiring professional medical help and home care services.

9. Long-term care options
When a parent is no longer able to care for himself or herself at home, you may need to look for some type of long-term care facility. There are many options available ranging from retirement communities to nursing homes. Choosing which one is right for you and your parent can be a difficult decision. Be conscious of your parent's needs, the location of the facility, the caregiver's reputation, and your budget. Consider a variety of options before you commit to one.

10. Legal documents
Talk to your parents about writing out legal documents such as wills and healthcare directives. Wills are used in the case of death, whereas healthcare directives are legal documents to communicate your parents' wishes for healthcare in the event that they cannot communicate. Writing such a directive will help them keep control of their lives and what happens to them in case of an emergency. You and other family members should know the location of such documents. Taking care of these arrangements and

Figure 13.4   Sample educational content for Financial $Lifeline.
SOURCE: Mitch Anthony.

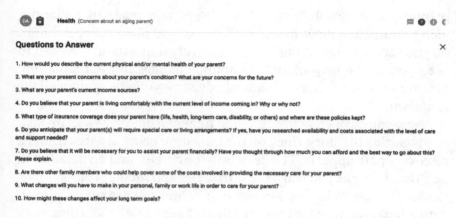

Figure 13.5 Sample discover path for discussion for Financial $Lifeline.
SOURCE: Mitch Anthony.

The Ongoing Conversation—Life Unfolding

As you begin to start the conversation around transitions, you soon realize that this is the piece of discovery that is never finished, because life keeps happening. Whether you use a systemized process is up to you. Obviously, we have a bias around that issue and would encourage you to bring discipline and more granularity to the life-unfolding conversation. One of the resulting dynamic changes is that the client's unfolding life story occupies center stage in the planning process. Another shift that focusing on transitions brings to the relationship is the idea of the "Year in Preview" instead of the "Year in Review" (the focus that has driven the conversation in the past). There is nothing we can do to change what's happened in the last 12 months, but there is plenty we can do in the next 12 months in terms of preparing for what is ahead for the client. The client intuitively understands the idea that *it is better to repair than to prepare.*

Any planner that neglects this conversation does so at his or her own risk. When teaching transitions dialogues, Mitch often cautions planners with the warning that, if you're not proactively addressing life transitions, you run the risk of losing the business to the financial professional who is. Once, after teaching a two-day course on life-centered financial planning, one of the participants told Mitch about a client who was leaving him for another adviser. The adviser called the departing client and asked what was happening:

> "Well I just received an inheritance and I've been talking to someone else about it, and they're going to help me."
> "May I ask how much the inheritance was?"
> "Just over $900,000."
> "How long have you been aware it was coming?"
> "Quite some time."
> "It's interesting; I just took a class and our instructor told us that if we weren't aware of the transitions happening in our clients' lives, that we ran the risk of losing those clients."
> "Yep," this client responded—and that was the end of that conversation and advisory relationship.

Cause or Effect

Given the choice of addressing an effect or a cause, a strategic thinker would always prefer the latter. Addressing the effect puts you in a position of continually putting out fires, thereby limiting the capacity for controlling the situation. Yet, in observing the general practices of the financial advice industry, the majority of practitioners are highly reactive instead of proactive when it comes to the majority of life transitions facing their clients (with the exception of the few transitions noted above).

One study showed that if you want a client to entrust their retirement assets to you, then you need to start the conversation four and a half years ahead of that particular transition. We think there is a principle at work here with all transitions in life. If you're waiting until the event happens, you're chasing the effect (money in motion) instead of the cause (the life transition).

Positioning your practice dialogues around the life course of the client is simply wisdom at work. Most clients make their biggest mistakes in the midst of major life transitions. By being proactive about the changes you know are coming, you can help clients avoid these mistakes. Think of it as *life event risk management*.

What could be more personal than a financial plan that is prefaced with the actual life map of the client in front of you? That is the most meaningful dialogue any client could hope for. Your clients will see the direct connection between their situation and their financial decisions.

"Take no thought for tomorrow. Sufficient for today is the evil thereof." These famous words from the Sermon on the Mount make for good guideposts for an effective inaugural and "year in preview" client dialogue. As we've stated before, there is a time and place for a "goals" conversation; but the time is not until after all of today's concerns have been surfaced and addressed. Dig deep enough into the here and now ... and you'll find no trouble making connections for the sweet by and by.

Chapter 14
Retirement Reframed

If you think going to the Moon is hard, try staying home.
—Eugene Cernan, retired NASA astronaut

A few years back Mitch met an extremely wealthy and recently retired entrepreneur. This man had invented carbon fiber, had a long and prosperous run in business, and retired at the age of 76. When he and Mitch met six months after their initial meeting, he told Mitch, "In your book *The New Retirementality* you said I should look for a retirement coach. Well, I've looked all over my state and can't find *one!* I'm six months into this thing, and I'm going crazy."

It was then that Mitch knew it was time to create a template for retirement coaching that advisers could deliver. The adviser's office is the most common place that the retirement discussion comes up, and you are in a position to make a huge difference in many clients' lives simply by broadening the dialogue around retirement from numbers only to lifestyle first and numbers second:

"Mr. and Mrs. Client, we really need to answer two big questions regarding retirement:

1. How are you going to spend your time, and
2. How are you going to pay for it?"

The second question can't be answered until the first one is. This context-opening script will help you gain the permission needed to engage in a life-centered retirement conversation. In this chapter, we will lay out that conversation and feature some of the tools we've created to help clients think through the lifestyle implications of retirement.

Not all people retire well, and there is something we can do about this.

Individually Speaking

Some people can't retire soon enough: their workplace, their coworkers, and their workload are literally killing them. On the other end of the spectrum, some people will never retire because who they are and what they do are inextricably amalgamated. They feel a calling around what they do, and to remove them from that calling is to lose their very breath of life. Then there are those individuals of all descriptions between these two extreme examples. Each person needs to work out a plan for life that best suits them.

These are the four major aspects to the retirement coaching dialogue:

1. Retirement observations: What have they observed watching others retire?
2. Visioning: Those that retire *to* something feel much better than those who retire *from* something.
3. Examination of work: What lifestyle benefits were they deriving from their work, and how will they replace these benefits in their life?
4. Personal DNA: How will their natural personality wiring play out in this phase of life?

Retirement Staging

The old "one and done" retirement decision and subsequent leap off the employment cliff has been displaced with a more tiered or phased approach to retirement. This idea came to the fore a decade ago after the release of a Rand study, *Unretirement*, that stated: "The prevalence of un-retirement, as well as partial retirement, underscores the rising importance of multi-stage retirement transitions, not only as the outcome of uncertain realizations of the budget constraint after retirement, but also possibly through dynamic preferences for leisure."[1]

We need to pay attention to the phrase "multi-stage," as it indicates that most retirees will require two to four attempts to achieve the balance and fulfillment they seek at the many different levels in life. It is not a one-and-done decision. This study concluded that it takes people three to four attempts to arrive at the sort of balance they seek in this stage of life. We believe that balance is finding the personal sweet spot between vacation and vocation.

Here's how we suggest framing the dialogue with your clients:

"Mr. and Mrs. Client, something we've discovered around retirement is that it takes most people three to four attempts to find the right balance of life. We're going to suggest that we split this conversation into four stages:

1. Looking Forward: Somewhere between two to five years ahead of the transition.
2. On the Cusp: Within six months of your retirement date.
3. Honeymoon: Six months into the transition.
4. Reality Check: One and a half years into retirement."

Step 1: Observing

How do you and your clients avoid the deleterious impact of retirement? How can you help them avoid "retirement whiplash"— where reality catches up with them all of a sudden? How do you help clients become aware of both their concerns and their hopes heading into retirement? The Retirement Observations Checklist (figure 14.1) is designed to help facilitate this conversation. We recommend it as the launchpad conversation in the retirement coaching process.

Everyone has some experiences and observations they've stored away in their memory banks about a family member, neighbor, or coworker who made an impression on them. We feel it's important for the life-centered financial planner to be aware of these observations. Once your clients have shared their observations, you've earned the space to share your personal observations about what you've seen in those who retire well and those who don't. Think this through for yourself and be ready to share a distilled version of your many observations along these lines. The dialogue introduction can go something like this:

> "Mr. and Mrs. Client, we've all made mental notes as we've watched family and friends enter into retirement. This checklist is designed to help you think through both your concerns and hopes as you head into retirement."

Step 2: Visioning

The second aspect of the life-centered retirement coaching process is to have clients begin thinking about what they hope to extract out of life ahead. Most people spend more time planning a two-week vacation than they do a 30-year retirement. Somehow, they must think meaningful activity will just fill space, and everything will work itself out. Yet, they would never allow such whimsical and laissez-faire thinking about their Caribbean vacation plans. The Visioning Tool (figure 14.2) can help get this conversation started.

Once your client has had the opportunity to articulate their vision for the period ahead, you can help them figure out how to monetize that vision. We've all learned that it's important to have a bucket list to pursue—it's also important to have something on the agenda ahead. Once we exhaust our bucket list, there's little left to do but kick the bucket.

My Retirement Observations

Directions: Below are the attributes you have witnessed in those who have retired well and those who have not. In column one, choose the attributes that concern you; in column two, choose the attributes that you've observed.

Attributes of Those Who Have Not Retired Well
(Check all that you've observed)

☐ Lack of challenges

☐ Boredom

☐ No (or not enough) hobbies

☐ No social network

☐ Marital strain

☐ Trouble adapting

☐ Feeling isolated

☐ Loss of identity

☐ Intellectual decline

☐ Lack of structure

☐ Upended plans

☐ Health issues

☐ Loss of spouse or partner

☐ Not enough savings

☐ Fear of spending money

Attributes of Those Who Have Retired Well
(Check all that you've observed)

☐ Active bucket list

☐ Community engagement

☐ Robust network

☐ Active social life

☐ Work (at least part-time)

☐ Fulfilling hobbies

☐ Routines

☐ Purpose-driven activities

☐ Well thought-out plan

☐ Positive family relationships

☐ Coaching/mentoring

☐ Physical activity

☐ Supporting a cause

☐ Having enough savings

☐ Still challenging self

Figure 14.1 Retirement observations checklist.
SOURCE: Mitch Anthony.

Visioning

Our VISIONING PROCESS in the 24 Things to do in Retirement exercise will help you get a clearer picture of what you want to experience in the rich years ahead.

Directions: Choose 6 images (below) that fit your vision for retirement.

Figure 14.2   Visioning tool.
SOURCE: Mitch Anthony.

Step 3: Working

> If your only reason for doing what you do
> Is to have enough money
> To no longer have to do it,
> What will you do,
> When you're done?
>
> You may find
> That a big part of you
> Was in the doing
> And that an important part
> Is undone.
>
> A job may be finished
> But the piece of you
> That does the work
> Is never done.

Too many retirees come to the realization of the actual lifestyle benefits of work too late to do anything about it. A significant number of retirees often wish they had delayed, phased in, or not retired at all. Having a candid conversation about work and its benefits has been and can be a game changer for many, if not most clients.

Intellectual capital—what you know, how well you know it, street savvy, know-how, know-who, rainmaking relationships, contextual understanding, history and strategic insight—is a valuable commodity.

How do you turn all this off at retirement? And once you do, how do the businesses and institutions recover from the loss of such precious capital? What's between your ears is what makes the world of business go 'round. Every institution, whether it's for profit or not, relies heavily on the intellectual and experiential capital of its members. This sort of capital is not easily replaced and has worth in two ways: (1) it brings in money when you know how to get it done and who to work with, and (2) it benefits your sense of personal esteem to exercise this capital on an ongoing basis.

Let's not lose sight of Maslow's hierarchy here. The second-to-last step (before self-actualization) is *esteem*. Once we stop utilizing our intellectual capital, we abandon a source of esteem that has served us throughout our professional lives. What well will you tap esteem from next? I'll never forget the retired physician who told me about the time he was stopped on the street and asked, "Didn't you used to be Dr. Jones?"

He went from "who's who" to "who's he?" in a heartbeat.

We suggest having a conversation about your clients' work, their intellectual capital, and the things they do to fuel their personal esteem and expression. You might find many a willing participant for this discussion in the professional ranks. Age has nothing to do with it, because it's all about what people bring to the game and how long they want to play. There's nothing wrong with going from being a starting player to a role player in the next phase of life, just as long as clients still feel they have some game. The Retirement Worksheet (figure 14.3) is designed to help facilitate this conversation by having clients rank the lifestyle and economic benefits of work.

Upon completing the profile, the client often experiences one or more personal epiphanies, including the importance of at least some work-related motivators and the fact that lifestyle factors (1–10 in figure 14.3) ranked higher than economic ones (11–20 in figure 14.3). For most of us, there's more to work than the money.

The Rand study we mentioned earlier talked about "*preference shocks,*" where many individuals found retirement less satisfying than anticipated. Surprisingly, the study found that unfulfilled work expectations were much more common than unfulfilled leisure ones.

The bottom line is that the retirement pitch for the last generation has headlined the benefits of leisure, but those who enter into it full time are finding that leisure alone cannot deliver the life satisfaction they seek. The exclusively life-of-leisure retirement is a mirage.

Mitch has been beating this drum for the last two decades. Individuals migrating from full-time contributors to full-time consumers cannot help but feel an existential shock to their systems.

Retirement WORKsheet

*Look at the following list of Reasons for Working and rank them 1-5
(with 1 being the lowest and 5 being the highest) in order of importance to you.*

1. Intellectual stimulation	1	2	3	4	5
2. To stay healthy	1	2	3	4	5
3. Social engagement	1	2	3	4	5
4. Enjoyment of competing	1	2	3	4	5
5. Fear of boredom	1	2	3	4	5
6. Growth and learning	1	2	3	4	5
7. Making an impact	1	2	3	4	5
8. Sense of relevance	1	2	3	4	5
9. Identity tied to my work	1	2	3	4	5
10. Talents and abilities are expressed through my work	1	2	3	4	5
11. Maintaining my lifestyle	1	2	3	4	5
12. Employer-sponsored benefits package	1	2	3	4	5
13. Money for extras	1	2	3	4	5
14. Can't afford to quit	1	2	3	4	5
15. Concerned about Social Security earnings restrictions	1	2	3	4	5
16. Would like to have more savings	1	2	3	4	5
17. Would like to pay down debt	1	2	3	4	5
18. Want to avoid drawing down assets	1	2	3	4	5
19. Have more to leave for heirs	1	2	3	4	5
20. Concerns about rising costs of living	1	2	3	4	5

Lifestyle Motivators: Add your total from numbers 1-10 = _____

Economic Motivators: Add your total from numbers 11-20 = _____

	0	10	15	20	25	30	35	40	45	50
Lifestyle Motivators										
Economic Motivators										

Figure 14.3 The retirement worksheet.
SOURCE: Mitch Anthony.

Self-indulgence is a poor prescription for a satisfying life. When some self-indulgence is balanced by service, relationship building, and exercise of aptitudes, it becomes a completely different story—with a much happier ending.

We've heard the financial concerns for years. What we hear less about are the nonfinancial retirement challenges that people have been colliding into in their retirement experiments:

Sense of identity loss: You were Dr. Jones for 40 years. Who are you now?

Social/relationship challenges: What if you actually enjoyed those people you were calling on?

Change/reduction in mental stimulation: Can Sudoku fill the bill?

Psychological issues around not getting a paycheck: Inflation can quickly make you paranoid about going to a movie.

Extra time to fill in the day: Are you wandering around the garage looking for something to break so you have something to fix?

Anxiety/depression: She (or he) doesn't seem too thrilled to have you around 24/7, does she (or he)?

These are the realistic, existential risks of retirement that humans must wrestle with. Add to these the concerns about money, inflation, and uncertainty in our markets, and it is no wonder that more and more people are coming to the same conclusion—*it works to work.* We do not mean to suggest that full-time work is required, but instead that individuals need only work as much as needed to meet their emotional, social, and intellectual stimulation needs. It will be different for every individual. Some may meet these needs in 10 hours of volunteering a week, whereas others may never slow their full-time work week until they completely expire—for the simple reason that *their work energizes them.* Isn't this the stuff of life?

We need to leave artificial visions of fulfilled retirements behind and embrace the human side of the equation. Our financial needs are only one piece in this puzzle. Take a look at the top four reasons

people gave for continuing their work.[2] Note that only one of four
has to do with money:

Staying healthy (90%)
Money for extras (87%)
Staying socially active (82%)
The challenge (79%)

Clearly, being challenged and active are now being mined not
only for longevity purposes but for quality of existence as well.
Advisers across our continents are seeing this trend play out and are
searching for a greater understanding of the trend and efficacious
methods for conversing on the topic. We're convinced you'll find
much fruitful dialogue in the work discussion.

Step 4: Personalization

Retirement is wonderful
If you have two essentials:
Much to live for, and
Much to live on.

–Anonymous

The fourth base of the life-centered retirement coaching dialogue is,
"How will your personality play itself out in retirement?" We are all
wired uniquely; one retirement plan does not fit all. One area that
should concern all of us is the rising divorce rates among retirees,
especially in the first 18 months of retirement. Clearly expectations
are not syncing up with reality. The next dialogue tool was created to
address the "couple's conundrum" to try to obviate the issue before
it gets too far entrenched. We are wired how we are wired, and that
wiring doesn't magically get rearranged because we turn 65 or stop
working. The My Retirementality Profile (figure 14.4) is designed as
a self-discovery exercise to see how a client's personality will best
play itself out in retirement.

My Retirementality™ Profile

Directions: *Within each group, choose the phrase that best describes you, with 4 being the most accurate and 1 being the least accurate. Total each letter on the bottom of the page. Do not leave any spaces blank, and be sure each group has a 1, 2, 3 and 4 rating.*

SAMPLE	
A	3
B	1
C	4
D	2

A___I love to kick back and relax.
B___I love to spend time with family and friends.
C___I love exercising.
D___I love my work.

A___I want to spend more time on hobbies and other interests.
B___I want time to travel.
C___I want to exercise more.
D___I want to continue to do the work I do.

A___I want to get away from work.
B___I want to spend more time with my spouse.
C___I want to expand my interests.
D___I want to continue doing what I do for the rest of my life.

A___I want to visit a lot of places.
B___I want to catch up with a lot of friends.
C___I want to make staying healthy a priority.
D___I want to continue competing and finding new challenges.

A___I look forward to "every day is Saturday."
B___I look forward to spending more time with the people who are important to me.
C___I look forward to more personal growth.
D___I look forward to interacting with people I work with.

A___I want to play every day.
B___I want to plan some family trips.
C___I want to pay more attention to my well-being.
D___I want to use my abilities to help others.

A___I want to start working on my "bucket list."
B___I want to start making memories.
C___I want to focus on being in top shape.
D___I want to make a difference in the world.

A___I want to wake up to an empty agenda.
B___I want to be more involved in the community.
C___I want to increase my energy level.
D___I want to feel challenged on a daily basis.

A___I have many interests that take up my time.
B___I look forward to spending time with friends.
C___I want to lower my stress level.
D___I want to continue being able to use my skills.

A___Free time is my top priority.
B___I want to invest in relationships.
C___I want to find some balance.
D___I am completely engaged in what I do professionally.

Add up totals for each and record in the box below.

TOTALS: A = [ ]   B = [ ]   C = [ ]   D = [ ]

Figure 14.4 My Retirementality profile.
SOURCE: Mitch Anthony.

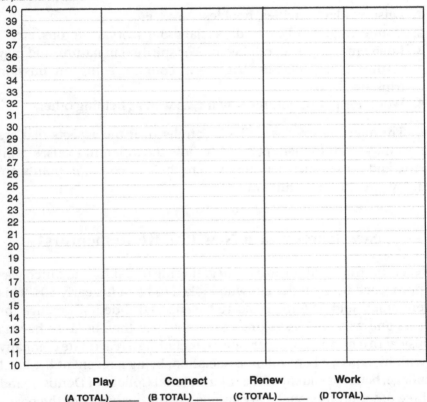

My Retirementality™ Profile

Directions: Once you've totaled your findings, graph your "A" total in the Play column, "B" total in the Connect column, "C" total in the Renew column, and "D" total in the Work column. Draw a line to connect the dots. The results will help you and your advisor determine what is important to you and how to integrate your profile into your plans for the future.

	Play	Connect	Renew	Work
	(A TOTAL)_____	(B TOTAL)_____	(C TOTAL)_____	(D TOTAL)_____

Graph scale: 40 down to 10

LEGEND

A. **PLAY** = LEISURE, TRAVEL, HOBBIES

B. **CONNECT** = TIME FOR FAMILY/FRIENDS

C. **RENEW** = PHYSICAL/MENTAL WELL-BEING

D. **WORK** = PROFESSION, HELPING OTHERS

Figure 14.4 (*Continued*)

Couples can fill out the profile individually and then plot their answers together on a grid to see where their wires cross or fray. Think of it as Myers and Briggs meets retirement.

There are four basic focuses that are common as people enter the retirement phase:

1. Leisure: play activities, hobbies, travel, etc.
2. Connecting: family, friends, social groups, organizations, etc.
3. Renewing: physical, intellectual, or spiritual in nature, and may involve taking classes, beginning courses, going on mission trips, etc.
4. Work: for pay or volunteer work, as well as helping others.

Through this exercise, clients can discover the aspects that are most important to them personally, how the different focuses compare, and for couples, learning where their in-common points are and where they are different.

New Heroes for a New Era: Retirementors

Recently after speaking to a client gathering in California, Mitch was approached by a gentleman who looked to be in his early 50s. This gentleman told Mitch he had run a successful dental practice for years and was now just showing up now and then because he was busy with a number of other causes, including a real estate company (with his sons), a benevolent association, being a regent at the local college, being president of the International College of Dentists (and three other professional associations), being chairman of the board of a local bank, and more.

This doctor told Mitch that through the years he has returned to his home village in China to build a school, a modern water system, and a temple. Stunned at his productivity for someone in his 50s, Mitch asked him how old he was. "I'm 83," he responded, "and I think I have a lot of good years left. I appreciate very much your message because I think many people have many more good years than they think if they will stay with it."

Mitch was both amazed and full of awe. At 83, this man looked like he was 53, had the articulation of a talk-show host, the perspicacity and acuity of a surgeon, the energy of a start-up entrepreneur, and the unmistakable shine in the eye of a man who not only made his own way in the world, but also made his own finish line as well.

Clearly traditional retirement images don't fit all who are considering retirement today.

This gentleman is an example of people we refer to as *retirementors*—people who are redefining what retirement is. We suggest that you form your own *Retirementors Council* within your practice: a group of clients you've handpicked who have come to a place of purpose, fulfillment, and balance-in-life in retirement. Think about hosting an event once a year or so where aspiring retirees could ask these retirementors about the challenges and joys of retirement. Why not tap the intellectual and experiential capital within your client base to the advantage of your younger clients?

For those of you curious to know more on this topic, we suggest reading Mitch's book, *The New Retirementality* (now in its fifth edition). The book was written for your clients and discusses how retirement is different for everyone. The book warns readers not to let preconceived notions and clichés about retirement dictate their decisions. For those of you who seek to be more competent and equipped retirement coaches, we suggest visiting Retirementcoachingprogram.com where you'll find digital coaching tools (like those featured in this chapter) and marketing and educational resources to help you become your community's go-to retirement coach.

Notes

1. M. E. von Bonsdorff, K. S. Shultz, E. Leskinen, and J. Tansky, "The Choice between Retirement and Bridge Employment: A Continuity Theory and Life Course Perspective." *International Journal of Aging and Human Development* 69 (2009): 79–100.

2. BAI and Financial Research Corporation, "2009 Retirement Study: Capitalize on Market Opportunities," October 2009. www.frcnet.com/documents/2009-BAI-FRC-Retirement-Study-Fact-Sheet.pdf.

Chapter 15

Personal Values and Account Values

... of what story or stories do I find myself a part?
—*Alasdair MacIntyre,* After Virtue: A Study in Moral Theory,
Third Edition

Mitch was recently invited to a think tank hosted by Eventide Asset Management, a company in the values investing space. CIO Finny Kuruvilla gave a talk where he found himself personally confronted with the question, "Do you want to own companies that you are proud of?"

Of course we do, don't we? But truth be told, most us haven't been paying attention. Kuruvilla defined good corporations as those who treated their workers well, who in turn engendered happy clients, demonstrated community mindedness, environmental responsibility, and more—in short, companies that produce goods and services for the good of the people. Sounds easy but it's not. The degree of due diligence required is onerous and ongoing, and the indicators are not always obvious.

We see a broad range of values-driven investment choices today including, but not limited to:

SRI (socially responsible investing)
ESG (environmental, social, governance)
BRI (biblically responsible investing)

There is also a whole subset of investment choices driven by the "Would I be proud to own them?" question:

"Would I want to work for them?"
"Would I recommend their products?"
"Would I want my kid to work there?"
"Would Grandma approve of their working conditions and atmosphere?"
"What value do they bring?" (There's a broad range of value out there from new flavors of bubble gum to potential cancer cures.)

Some companies strive to deliver value, while others exist only to extract value. Extractors are the companies that the ESG movement is trying to weed out. Why would any of us want to support firms that don't care about anything or anyone? In his book, *The Ultimate Question*, Bain Fellow and author Fred Reichheld, of Bain Consulting, said the following about those companies:

> Instead of focusing on innovations to improve value for customers, they channel their creativity into finding new ways of extracting value from customers. In short, companies regard the people who buy from them as their adversaries, to be coerced, milked, or manipulated as the situation permits. The Golden Rule—treat others as you would like to be treated—is dismissed as irrelevant in a competitive world of hardball tactics. Customers are simply a means to an end—fuel for the furnace that forges superior profits. This view is utter nonsense. Companies that let themselves be brainwashed by such a philosophy are headed into the sinkhole of bad profits, where true growth is impossible.[1]

Scrambled Signals

In our modern age of inclined growth of values-screened investing, people could be forgiven if they suffered from a degree of incredulity on the difficulty of getting to the core of truth in corporations and their actual behaviors. Don't all corporations try to say the right things, give the proper appearance, and elevate their standing in the global community? Don't values range wildly from one individual to another, and from one credo, culture, and affiliation to the next?

As a case in point, consider the fact that one ESG data vendor gave Phillip Morris a higher ESG score than Loxo Oncology Corporation for the simple reason that the weightier screens applied to the test were clean water and board diversity. Rather ironic that the tobacco company produces the products that science has proven cause cancer, while Loxo has gone to market with a potential cure—yet the causative party is rated higher in ethics, sustainability, and governance than the curative party. Excuse us while we scratch our heads for a moment and wonder how "values" have become so perplexingly scrambled. According to an executive at this gathering, one of the big weaknesses with ESG historically is that it does not consider the products/services of the companies, but instead focuses on their sustainability "practices."

In an article in *Investment News*, titled "How to Spot Greenwashing,"[2] Jeff Benjamin points out that for ESG to be sustainable over time, more fund managers are going to need to raise their levels of due diligence to see if companies are actually engaging in healthy practices or simply giving their firms a green veneer with propaganda and superfluous remedies. Another issue he pointed out is the need for the inspection and reporting of statistics to be validated. Benjamin asserted that the ideal scenario would be for the firm to have active engagement and collaborating dialogue with individual companies. We're not there yet but suspect that we will soon see progress in the filtering process as well.[3]

Locate Your Values

Everyone has to choose what matters most to them personally. The firm that hosted the think tank had set their searchlights on companies making a much-needed stride in healthcare, cybersecurity, and clean water (among other things) around the planet. They had invested in a company that came up with a new treatment for schizophrenia, which is a (if not the) leading contributor to homelessness, that impacts 3 million people in the United States.

Mitch learned that 1.6 million people a year die from diarrhea, and over 80% of them are under the age of 5. This is due to unclean water that could be corrected in a few short years via proper infrastructure. He learned that cybersecurity breaches cost over $2 trillion a year, and the leading victims are the elderly and retired. It's hard for any of us not to care about these issues. Is it possible that we can care with our investment dollars and turn a profit as well? Is there a sweet spot between humans flourishing and profitability that is begging for our vigilance and participation?

What matters to you? What matters to your clients? How much longer can we ignore these questions or patronize the issue with superficial discovery questions like, "Are there any stocks or companies you'd like to avoid?" I don't say this to denigrate the value of such a question but to illustrate the idea that being *against* certain products (think "sin" stocks) is a valid inquiry, but the conversation will need, at some point, to move from "What are you against?" to "What are you for?"

The Time Is upon Us

I suspect that your clients are hungering for such a conversation *right now*. I suspect that today's clients are keen on the idea of *alignment* between their personal values and account values. Are you ready to bring it?

One adviser who is ahead of the curve on this issue is Jeffrey Gitterman, who serves clients in the New York City and New Jersey regions. His clients are largely college professors who are amenable to the conversation of aligning their assets with their views. Gitterman has been bold and intentional, and in 18 months moved every dollar under management into the ESG arena. Not a single client said no to the idea. Gitterman, who has emerged as a thought leader and a leading advocate in the ESG space, told Mitch, "88% of clients surveyed want to have this conversation and only 6% of advisers are engaged in the conversation. What pool do you want to be swimming in? Where all of the advisers are and no clients are, or where all of the clients are and no advisers are present?"

I've tracked Jeffrey Gitterman's career for many years and know that he's been very successful and that his key driver has always been the well-being of his clients. Maybe we could all learn something from his example. After all, when is the last time you presented an idea to clients that got a 100% positive and active response?

Righteous Profits, Happy World

It just makes sense to reward companies that reward their employees, their communities, and the world at large. Obviously these ESG screens and filters cannot be agnostic to profits. It stands to reason that if a company treats their workers, clients, communities, and the environment well, then profits would respond in kind. To quote King Solomon, one of the wealthiest individuals to ever live, "When the righteous prosper, the city rejoices" (Proverbs 11:10, NIV). When business is done the right way for all involved, then all are somehow beneficiaries of the product or service well done. We heard a phrase on values-based investing that we had never heard before: "Investing that makes the world rejoice." We're all happy to turn a profit—we'd be all the happier to know that we turned a profit properly and on principle.

It boggles the mind that as a society we seek to align our values in almost every aspect of life—how we raise our children, how we vote, whom we work for, where we give our money—but not so much with our hard-earned savings. Imagine walking your 18-year-old-child to the front door and saying, "I don't care how you do it, just go out there and bring back as much money as you can."

Which of us would give a large check to a random charity and say, "We're not concerned with what you do, just give us a receipt for our donation."

Most of us would never act this way, but yet when it comes to our investments, we do. In the past, this mode of operation has been unwitting. That is no longer the case. From this point forward, we will be either witting participants or willfully negligent.

This is a conversation that is just beginning. Awareness is growing. We would all do well to take the time to get educated enough to be able to translate the possibilities to clients and to give them investment choices that will do their souls—not to mention their account balances—some good.

One way to raise the percentage of advisers engaging in the investment values conversation is to incorporate some sort of survey or self-reflection exercise into our discovery protocols. Mitch has developed a simple inventory to get this process and conversation going called the Investor Values Inventory (exhibit 15.1).

Exhibit 15.1: Investor Values Inventory

This inventory is a self-discovery instrument designed to help you understand the correlation between your deeply held personal values and your monetary investments. Answer each question according to your personal rationale and convictions.

Monetary Questions

Choose 1 for "least likely" and 5 for "most likely."

If you got a return of 10% from blindly investing and 10% from investing in companies that reflected your values, how likely would you be to move more assets into the values investing category?

1_____2_____3_____4_____5

What percentage of your investments would you be willing to invest in this values investing category?

10%____20%____30%____40%____50%____Other _____

If you got a return of 10% from blindly investing and 7% from investing in companies that reflected your values, how likely would you be to move more assets into the values investing category?

1_____2_____3_____4_____5

What percentage of your investments would you be willing to invest in this values investing category?

10%____20%____30%____40%____50%____Other _____

If you got a return of 7% from blindly investing and 10% from investing in companies that reflected your values, how likely would you be to move more assets into the values investing category?

1_____2_____3_____4_____5

What percentage of your investments would you be willing to invest in this values investing category?

10%____20%____30%____40%____50%____Other _____

If you got a return of 7% from blindly investing and 6% from investing in companies that reflected your values, how likely would you be to move more assets into the values investing category?

1_____2_____3_____4_____5

(continued)

(*continued*)

What percentage of your investments would you be willing to invest in this values investing category?

10%____20%____30%____40%____50%____Other _____

If you got a return of 10% from blindly investing and 5% from investing in companies that reflected your values, how likely would you be to move more assets into the values investing category?

1_____2_____3_____4_____5

What percentage of your investments would you be willing to invest in this values investing category?

10%____20%____30%____40%____50%____Other _____

General Questions

Choose 1 for "least agreement with" and 5 for "most agreement with."

I have some very specific values that I would not violate in return for investment profits.

1_____2_____3_____4_____5

If I discovered that I owned investments that violated my principles, I would redirect those monies.

1_____2_____3_____4_____5

I don't wish to invest in companies that are producing products that are proven to be unhealthy.

1_____2_____3_____4_____5

Environmental Questions

Choose 1 for "least agreement with" and 5 for "most agreement with."

Taking care of our natural resources should take precedent over producing profits.

1_____2_____3_____4_____5

I would not invest in companies that have a record of polluting the environment.

1_____2_____3_____4_____5

I would be much more inclined to invest in companies with a "green" track record.

1_____2_____3_____4_____5

Employees Questions

Choose 1 for "least agreement with" and 5 for "most agreement with."

Employee morale is something that corporate leaders should be focused on.

1_____2_____3_____4_____5

I would not invest in companies that have a record of treating employees badly.

1_____2_____3_____4_____5

(continued)

(*continued*)

Companies that treat employees well are more likely to have satisfied customers as well.

1_____2_____3_____4_____5

Governance Questions

Choose 1 for "least agreement with" and 5 for "most agreement with."

Companies have a social responsibility to care for and support the communities they live in.

1_____2_____3_____4_____5

CEOs that produce profits at the expense of employee well-being should be fired.

1_____2_____3_____4_____5

I would want to invest in companies that work hard at improving their communities.

1_____2_____3_____4_____5

Customers Questions

Choose 1 for "least agreement with" and 5 for "most agreement with."

I would be more likely to want to invest in companies that get high customer satisfaction ratings.

1_____2_____3_____4_____5

I would want to invest in companies that I personally recommend to my family and friends.

1_____2_____3_____4_____5

What percentage of your investments would you be willing to invest in the values investing category?

10%___20%___30%___40%___50%___Other _____

How important is each of the following to you?

1 Extremely unimportant
2 Unimportant
3 Neutral
4 Important
5 Extremely important

Companies should respect the value and freedom of all people by avoiding:
Abortive/contraceptives/stem cell research

1_____2_____3_____4_____5

Alcohol

1_____2_____3_____4_____5

Gambling

1_____2_____3_____4_____5

Tobacco

1_____2_____3_____4_____5

Companies should demonstrate a concern for justice and peace by avoiding:
Controversial weapons

1_____2_____3_____4_____5

(continued)

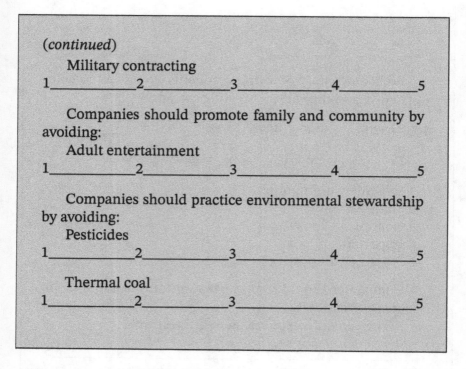

(continued)
   Military contracting
1_____2_____3_____4_____5

   Companies should promote family and community by avoiding:
   Adult entertainment
1_____2_____3_____4_____5

   Companies should practice environmental stewardship by avoiding:
   Pesticides
1_____2_____3_____4_____5

   Thermal coal
1_____2_____3_____4_____5

This inventory, available in electronic form through ROLAdvisor, can be adjusted to substitute a broader range of questions or those from a completely separate values category. The conversation that ensues should cover both monetary and values implications of the choices made.

You'll note that the tension in the monetary questions ranges from 1% (7–6) to 3% (10–7) to 5% (10–5) for the purpose of getting a handle on how pronounced a person's desire for alignment is, given a more negative return scenario. In the monetary question, assuming a higher return in the values space may appear to make the question seem too obvious to ask, but the real insight comes with the secondary question regarding what percentage of their assets a client would move into the values category given the higher return assumption. How they would weight future investing choices is another measure of their desire for alignment of beliefs and investments.

Even though we're making negative assumptions here to test the level of tension, the irony of this matter is that there are plenty of funds in this space delivering superior returns. Now, more than at any time before, we can see appreciative returns with appreciable social value.

Remember the first principle of life-centered financial planning? *Aligning means with meaning.* This is where the process starts. What matters to our client matters to us. We want them to experience the purity and beauty of knowing their assets are in an integral flow with their inner selves and deeply held priorities and principles.

Notes

1. Fred Reichheld. *The Ultimate Question* (Harvard Business School Press, 2006).
2. https://www.investmentnews.com/how-to-spot-greenwashing-188442.
3. For more information on efforts toward better ESG standards:
   Morningstar.com: Using data from Sustainalytics, Morningstar's globe rating system provides a historical sustainability score that includes metrics for carbon risk and fossil-fuel involvement. The globe ratings are updated monthly based on the latest portfolio reporting, and consider the trailing 12 months, while weighting recent portfolios more heavily.
   MSCI.com/ESG-ratings: MSCI is expanding its universe of funds that are screened and graded with ESG scores. The grading is on a seven-point scale and provides context as to specific ESG areas where the fund is strong, average, and weak.
   FossilFreeFunds.org: Part of AsYouSow.org: This screening tool provides detailed analysis of a fund's underlying holdings. In addition to a breakdown of fossil-fuel holdings, the site grades funds on factors including deforestation, gender equality, civilian firearms, military weapons, and tobacco.

Chapter 16
Enough Already ...

Money isn't the most important thing in the world, but it's high on the list, right up there with oxygen!

—Zig Ziglar

What's the ultimate aim of a financial planner? Contrary to what the industry would have us believe, it's not to beat the market. As we've said throughout the book, it's to help clients get and keep the life they want—to help them identify, achieve, and maintain their desired lifestyle without ever running out of money, or dying with too much. And because life is not a rehearsal, it's to help clients do the things they really want to do in the time they have left on this planet.

It's all about helping clients understand the answer to the big question: "How much is *enough*?" How much do they *really* need for the rest of their life? Or is it? The bigger question is, "Enough for what?"

And that's what life-centered financial planning is all about: understanding clients' lives and what they want to achieve. And so we end this book where we started; by answering that overarching question looming over financial advice: "*What's the money for in the first place?*" This is the one dynamic question that drives "enough."

The fact is, it's different for each of us. Only you know the cost of your lifestyle. But you need to know about the cost of your client's lifestyle! Remember, though, we're not talking here about creating a budget. Budgets aren't fun. A budget is where you spend the same

185

money this month as you did last month. That's a conversation no one is overly excited to engage in.

We're talking about helping clients design, create, and *keep* a life worth living. We're helping them get a handle on the cost of their lifestyle so they can plan to maintain it or make it better. If they haven't got a clue how much they spend, then it's time for you to give them a shake.

We believe that true financial independence is being in such a position that if you work beyond a certain date, it's because you want to, not because you have to. It's about having sufficient resources to maintain your future desired lifestyle without risk of ever running out of money.

It's about having *your* enough.

Keeping your desired lifestyle and not running out of money is the key.

You see, anyone can have a great lifestyle temporarily. All you need is half a dozen credit cards. Or better still, just keep re-mortgaging your house every few years. That is exactly what a large percentage of the population has been doing in recent years, helped, until recently, by easy access to credit.

For many years it has been easier for clients to take out a credit card and spend money they haven't got than it is for them to put money aside for their future. The trouble with the easy credit culture that so many people have gotten used to is that it creates a situation where many people can't afford the lifestyle they have now while they are still working—let alone when they stop work and the money stops coming in. Some people are just going to have to get used to living on less ... a lot less.

We're not suggesting for one minute that your clients' lifestyle and how much they spend is the most important thing in life. But when it comes to successfully planning their financial future, it definitely is the most important thing. Period. What's important is getting enough money to satisfy their needs. And that's where the problem starts.

What are your client's *real* needs? What do they really want? Helping clients to start thinking about their lifestyle, and the cost of maintaining it, can be an eye opener to something much deeper. Remember, we're not talking here about having more, more, more. We're talking about living big and living rich—according to how your client defines living.

Living rich can often be about *not* having more; it can actually be about having less. It can be about quitting that $400,000 a year job in the city (a job that perhaps no longer fulfils your client) to go and live in a small house in the country, earning very little but being really happy and fulfilled doing what they love. That's living rich.

People live big by following their heart and by following their passion. Living rich can mean devoting one's life to breeding a brand-new type of rose or teaching yoga classes or going on medical relief trips. The question is, what do your clients want their financial future to look like—in particular, their desired lifestyle? Only you can help them answer that.

Certain Uncertainties

One of the most common questions new clients have asked Paul in his years as a lifestyle financial planner is, "The trouble is, I don't really know what I want—so how can I plan my future?"

Paul's answer is simple: "You might not know what you want; few people do—and that's OK. But I'll bet that you do know what you *don't* want! And what you don't want is probably *nothing less than what you have right now*. Am I right?"

The starting point in creating any financial plan is to identify what clients have now; in other words, their current lifestyle. This becomes the starting point for planning the rest of their life and achieving financial independence. We can then plan to make adjustments to their lifestyle costs (perhaps in later life) through choice, rather than by being forced to make those changes.

To do this, we need to come to grips with what their current lifestyle looks like and how much it costs. We do this by going through a simple lifestyle expenditure questionnaire. This data can then help you look at the cost of various stages of their life, to see how it might change.

Planning your financial future successfully is all about waking up right now to the cost of the life we have. It's about comparing that to the life we want and the life we don't want—and understanding the costs of each.

This is the starting point in understanding how much is enough.

Three Types of Clients

Paul has been helping clients understand how much is enough for years. And one of the things he's noticed is that there are only three types of clients that financial planners can encounter: *Not Enough*, *Too Much*, and *Just Right*. Knowing which category your clients fall into is important because they each have different challenges.

Not Enough

As the name suggests, these are people who haven't yet got enough money to last their whole life. They are most definitely going to run out. More often, they are people who will never have enough unless they start accumulating wealth. They need desperately to know how much is enough.

Solving their problem is not as complicated as they might think. In simple terms, they probably need to increase the inflows, or they need to consider reducing their outflows (expenditure/lifestyle) now or in the future.

It's no crime to be a *Not Enough*. Millions of people are in this situation. It's not their fault. No one has ever helped them understand how to financially plan their future. No one has ever helped them work out how much is enough.

We blame the financial services industry. The industry has failed consumers; its leading interest was in selling financial products when really it should have been focused on answering these much bigger questions. The good news is this: it's easy to get clients to do something about it, and it doesn't have to be painful. They just need you to inspire them to face up to some truths and accept that certain things are going to have to go, now or in the future. Then, step by step, you can help them start doing something about it, so they accumulate enough to live the life they desire.

Got Too Much

As the name implies, these are people who have more than enough already or are heading that way. They are likely to go to their graves with *too much* money. That sounds like a nice sort of problem, but it's a problem, nonetheless.

Again, the answer is knowing how much is *enough* to last their whole life. Then, if there's going to be a surplus (because they're a *Got Too Much*), it opens up a whole host of possibilities. The biggest problem about being a *Got Too Much* is potentially becoming the richest man or woman in the graveyard. Nobody wants that. As the adage goes, "You can't take it with you."

Once clients truly understand how much is enough, you can help them plan their life accordingly. In particular, you can be a "giver of permission" by helping them spend more, live more, and give more—and feel good about it.

Remember, life is not a rehearsal. Now is your clients' chance to do stuff, while they still can. It's no good for your clients to be stuck in a wheelchair or in a nursing home wishing they had done more with their life when they had the chance.

Another good reason to spend now is that spending money is one of the best ways of reducing taxes on their estate. If a client spends more, they leave less for the tax man to take. But clients often need your reassurance—your permission. Or, perhaps they've done all they want with their life. They don't need or don't want to spend more. In that case, once they know how much is enough, they can start to feel really comfortable about giving money away.

Perhaps they could help their children and grandchildren or causes they deeply believe in. They'll feel really good about their choices because they'll know it's OK to share their wealth with others—they'll know it makes sense. Far better for clients to pass on money now when they are alive so they can actually see the benefit it brings to those they help. It is much more fulfilling to give with warm hands than cold ones.

Of course, it's also an opportunity to help good causes by leaving a legacy and creating something that lives on after they're gone. Once clients understand they *Got Too Much*, you can do something rather wonderful—something that will bring them more peace of mind.

You can help them reduce risk.

It never fails to amaze us how so many people who have more than enough money still stress and worry about it. More often than not, they invest in the wrong places, encouraged by the financial services industry. These clients often invest their money with a view of still trying to make more. Once clients come to realize they *Got Too Much*, you can help them start thinking about investing for prudence, instead of performance.

Why have wealth if it doesn't give you the life you want? Good question, don't you think? If you have clients who have the money, but not the life they hoped for, they are not affluent, they are *half-fluent*. Engaging in this particular conversation is exactly how you earn your stripes as a life-centered financial planner.

The Just Rights

Finally, there are the *Just Rights*. Imagine that you have more than enough money to last you for the rest of your life. You need never worry about money again. Financially, everything is perfect. You can keep living the life you want, and you're never going to run out of money. The only trouble is, because of the way the industry at large is programmed, you probably don't know it.

If your clients didn't know they were going to be OK, how would they live their lives? Chances are, they'd still worry about money. They would go without. They would skimp on the nice things in life. If they were still working, perhaps they would plan to retire at 68 when, in fact, 58 was possible. Perhaps they would keep working when they could be pursuing their bucket list. Perhaps they would be stressed out and tired, doing a job they no longer enjoyed, when instead, they could be doing something more fulfilling.

Do you have any clients who are already retired? Perhaps they worry about money and about how long it will last. Perhaps they aren't treating themselves or their family, even though they could easily afford to. Or worse, and this is very often the case, they might spend money—and then feel guilty for doing so. Imagine that...paying for a wonderful, once-in-a-lifetime holiday while thinking, "I shouldn't really be doing this!" That's no way to live. That's no way to have fun. Clients who are thinking and worrying about their money risk are missing the most important thing of all: the precious moment. Miss enough precious moments, and you miss a lifetime.

Here's another thought: clients would probably take more risks with their investments than they really need to. After all, they would always be seeking a good return on their money, easily falling prey to financial propaganda and all the financial scaremongering that fills newspapers and websites every day.

Worse, though, what about their precious time on this wonderful planet? If they didn't know they already had "enough," they would probably let opportunities pass them by. They wouldn't climb those mountains or sail those seas. They would probably never take that family trip to the islands they've always dreamed about. They wouldn't do stuff while they had the chance.

Then, sadly, they would eventually realize that they've become what Paul calls "too old to enjoy yourself" because their knees have gone, their hips have gone—and then they're in a wheelchair. And then they're dead. All this, because your client didn't realize that he or she had enough. There are millions of people who suffer from this problem, but your clients needn't be one of them. Again, the big questions are: *"How much is enough?"* driven by *"Enough for what?"* Your job is to help them find out.

There's a story Paul likes to share with clients called *The Mexican Boatman*. You may know it. We think it's important to bring this story to your attention as a life-centered financial planner. It's a great little story; so much so, that when Paul first heard it, he changed his personal definition of "success." Here's the story:

> There was a high-powered management consultant, who had a Harvard MBA. He was on holiday on a beach in Mexico. Early one morning he saw a local fisherman come up to the shore in his little boat. Inside the boat was a large yellow fin tuna. The consultant started talking to the fisherman and asked him, "Tell me, what you do with your life?"
>
> The fisherman responded, "Well, I go fishing early in the morning and catch a yellow fin tuna. I come back and sell it, and then go home, have breakfast or an early lunch with my beautiful wife. We chat a while. Most days we make love followed by a snooze in the afternoon. Then in the early evening, I play with the kids when they get back from school, I have dinner with my wife and then I go down to the local cantina where I play guitar, sing, and have a drink with my amigos!"
>
> The consultant said, "I think I can help you. I have a Harvard MBA. Here's my advice: instead of coming back so early, why don't you stay out and fish a little longer and catch more tuna. That way you can make more money so you can buy a bigger boat."
>
> "Really?" said the fisherman. "Then what happens?"
>
> "Well, then you can catch even more fish. Then you can employ some of your amigos and set up a fishing fleet to catch even more yellow fin tuna!"
>
> "Wow!" the fisherman exclaimed, "And then what happens?"
>
> "Well," said the consultant, "eventually, you can bypass the middleman completely and have your own cannery! Over the years you can build a fantastic fleet and a marvellous business!"
>
> The fisherman was fascinated by everything he was hearing: "That is brilliant; what happens next?"
>
> "Well, eventually, you'll have thousands of employees, you will have to move to a new headquarters in New York City. Then we'll help you do an IPO and sell the business and make millions!"
>
> "How many millions?"
>
> "Well ... about 20!"
>
> "Wow! 20 million! What happens then?"

"Oh, that is the best bit," the consultant responded. "You can then relax, retire to a little Mexican fishing village, and in the morning, you can get up and go fishing for a yellow fin tuna, and in the evening, you can play guitar and have a few drinks with your amigos!"

When Paul first heard that story, it stopped him in his tracks. He thought really hard about it.

It was one of those great lessons in life. He suddenly realized that he already had the success he was looking for. He had reached where he wanted to be. He just wasn't capitalizing and maximizing or thinking about the wonderful life that he already had. He got caught in the trap of wanting more, more, more.

The moral of the story is that your clients might already have the life they really want. So why grind harder or longer than they really need to? Life's too short.

Clients often lose sight of the big picture in the busyness of daily life. We can get so bogged down grinding through meaningless activities that we don't have time to think about what we really want to do with the time we have left. When we deliver life-centered financial planning, we can help our clients use their money to make a life instead of using their life to make money.

Life-centered financial planners understand that money isn't the most precious commodity of our existence ... time is.

Epilogue

The financial services industry at large has been encouraging our clients to ask the wrong questions when it comes to their money:

- How much did I earn on my investments?
- Do I have enough to retire?

These are the two most commonly asked questions. Instead of just asking, "How much did I earn?," what if we asked, "Am I managing my money in a way that improves my life?" Doesn't that get more to the point?

People will pull out a microscope to look at their investment return statement but apply a kaleidoscope to their own spending patterns. We see people who get a raise in their income immediately go out and leverage that raise to go further in debt. Is this managing money in a way that improves their life?

Instead of just asking, "Do I have enough to retire?" we should be encouraging them to ask, "Will I retire well?" This question applies to spirit, mind, body, and wallet. We've all witnessed far too many people enter retirement with plenty of assets but with poverty of purpose. Not only can they do better with their money, but they also can do much better with how they view their money.

It's important to remember that we are not only helping clients understand the answer to the question, "How much is enough?," we must also ask them to consider the bigger question, "Enough for what?" This is how you differentiate yourself.

Paul witnessed his father sacrifice family time in pursuit of "more"—all for the family, of course. He then observed his father's regret after losing his wife early. As a result, Paul made some life-changing decisions in his own life and literally set sail to a more fulfilling life.

Life is short. We all need to challenge many of our clients' assumptions about money and life. We can do better. We all need to go beyond the clichéd financial adviser who focuses solely on telling clients where they can garner the best returns. Instead, we need to help clients achieve a greater Return on Life.

Instead of asking people what they earn, Mitch often asks them, "How much is your paycheck costing you?" He has witnessed people change their careers in response to that question. This question may challenge you to make some changes as well—with money, with choices, with time, and most importantly, with the people you serve and the people who are precious to you.

You are working hard for what you have. Let's remind our clients (and ourselves) that life is not a rehearsal. We all sometimes act like we have forever, but we don't. Our precious time on this planet is slipping away, and the older we get, the faster time seems to go. We are here to remind clients of this fact and help them get what they want most—a life well lived.

Life does not consist of the things we own, regardless of how much we own. Life consists of living the best we can with what we have. This is the golden opportunity that lies before you as a life-centered financial planner.

Appendix

Return on Life™ (ROL) Manifesto

Professional financial advice has traditionally focused on helping you make and save more money. But lost in the shuffle was, "What's the money for?" The Return on Life™ (ROL) philosophy says money is still important but shifts the focus to putting your life at the center of the conversation. It's about helping you live the best life possible with the money you have.

Here are the beliefs that constitute the ROL approach:

1. *Money is simply a tool.* Money is not the goal, and it is not an end. It is a tool that we manage—exercising caution and wisdom—for the benefit of improving our clients' lives.
2. *Comparative measures are neither helpful nor necessary in making progress.* How an individual's returns compare to any index, fund, or investment category (relative investment performance) is inconsequential.
3. *Progress must be personalized.* Progress is best measured against an individual's own potential. For measures of progress to be effective, we must first establish a personal benchmark. This requires knowing where money is coming from and where money is going.

4. *The primary measure of success is Return on Life (ROL)*. The fundamental question in the ROL philosophy is not, "How much money do you need?" but rather, "Is your money being managed in a way that is improving your life?"

5. *How I am compensated is a matter of absolute transparency*. As a professional, I deliver value to my clients and make sure they understand what I offer and how I get paid.

6. *I can provide quality and value to a limited number of clients*. In order to serve others well by providing the greatest amount of value, and to keep my life in balance, I must choose to serve a reasonable number of clients.

7. *We are stewards of wealth, not owners*. Ultimately, everything I own will end up in the hands of others. With this understanding I pursue stewardship that recognizes the responsibility of supporting and securing personal, family, and community life.

8. *The greatest value I can bring to my clients is to bridge their means with their meaning*. I recognize the unique role I play between my clients' means and their sense of purpose and intention with their money.

9. *I will not entrust my clients' well-being to anyone who does not put my clients' interests ahead of their own*. I understand the sacred trust that exists in financial matters and will never refer my clients to anyone who does not appreciate this elevated level of trust.

10. *An ROL Adviser has a calling, not a job*. I understand that my commitment, passion, and devotion to help people improve their lives through wise financial decisions is more than just employment. It is a vital service that demands professionalism and intellectual, emotional, and spiritual investment of self.

About the Authors

Mitch Anthony and Paul Armson are the cofounders of www
.LifeCenteredPlanners.com, a fast-growing community
of advisers from around the globe who deliver or want to
get better at delivering life-centered financial planning.

Mitch Anthony

For almost two decades, Mitch has provided training and development for both individual advisers and major organizations throughout the world. Mitch personally consults with many of the largest and most recognizable names in the financial services industry on both life-centered financial planning and relationship development. He is the cofounder of ROLAdvisor.com and the founder of numerous nonprofit charitable organizations.

Mitch is a consistently top-rated presenter who speaks at major conventions around the globe and has been cited as one of the most meaningful speakers in financial services today. *Financial Planning* magazine named him one of the financial services industry's top "Movers & Shakers" for his pioneering work. He has also partnered with Texas Tech University to create the first life-centered financial planning certificate program.

Mitch is the author of many groundbreaking books for advisers and consumers, including perennial bestseller *StorySelling for Financial Advisors*, cited by *Financial Advisor* magazine as the number one "must-read" book for financial professionals. His other books include *The New Retirementality* (now in its fifth edition), *Defining Conversations*, *The Financial Professional's Storybook*, *Your Clients for Life*, *Your Client's Story*, *Selling with Emotional Intelligence,* and *The Financial Lit Kit* series of books (*The Cash in the Hat, The Bean Is Not Green,* and *Where Did the Money Go?*).

Mitch is a sought-after expert for the media and a regular columnist for *Financial Advisor* magazine. His columns have appeared on CBS MarketWatch and in the *Journal of Financial Planning*. His original comic strip "Stanley Brambles, CFG (Certified Financial Guru)" has appeared in *Research* magazine. Mitch is also host of the daily radio feature, The Daily Dose, heard on over 100 radio stations nationwide.

For more information about Mitch and his organization, visit www.mitchanthony.com or contact him at mitch@mitchanthony.com.

Paul Armson

Paul became a financial adviser in 1982. He started delivering Lifestyle Financial Planning to his clients in 1990 and built a small, but highly profitable fee-based financial planning practice focused primarily on helping small business owners and retirees.

After the sudden death of his mum, Paul vowed to make "life's not a rehearsal" his mantra and live life accordingly. He semiretired at the age of 45 to start sailing his yacht *Spellbound* around the world with his soulmate, Lynn.

When he's not sailing, Paul helps other financial advisers successfully transition to a life-centered financial planning model.

Paul launched www.inspiringadvisers.co.uk in 2013, as an easy-to-follow online training program to help advisers learn his methods in the comfort of their home or office. It is now a fast-growing community of life-centered (and lifestyle) financial planners from the UK and around the globe.

Paul is the author of three books, two for advisers: *The Financial Advisor's Survival Guide: How to Succeed and Prosper in a Fee Only World* and *The 7 Habits of Highly Successful Financial Planners: How to Really Matter in the Lives of Your Clients*. His book, *Enough? How Much Money Do You Need for the Rest of Your Life?* helps consumers understand the difference between financial planning and financial advice and educates them on what constitutes proper financial planning.

Paul is also the Founder of BACK2Y—The Lifestyle Financial Planning Conference in the UK that he supports without any sponsorship or backing from product providers or investment institutions. There are no free lunches. No free pens. No free golf balls. No free iPhone chargers. Paul believes that, in a fee-only world, advisers need to break the shackles of the financial industry and create a service proposition that does not rely on the sale or implementation of a financial product. Advisers need to get "back to why" they do the work they do: to take care of people and to help clients get and keep a great life.

Contact Paul at parmson@me.com.

Index